The American Historical
Imaginary

The American Historical Imaginary

Contested Narratives of the Past

CAROLINE GUTHRIE

Rutgers University Press

New Brunswick, Camden, and Newark, New Jersey, and London

Library of Congress Cataloging-in-Publication Data
Names: Guthrie, Caroline, author.
Title: The American historical imaginary : contested narratives of the past /
    Caroline Guthrie.
Description: New Brunswick, New Jersey : Rutgers University Press, [2023] |
    Includes bibliographical references and index.
Identifiers: LCCN 2022008510 | ISBN 9781978818804 (paperback) |
    ISBN 9781978818811 (hardback) | ISBN 9781978818828 (epub) |
    ISBN 9781978818842 (pdf)
Subjects: LCSH: History in popular culture—United States. | Mass media and
    history—United States. | National characteristics, American. | Walt Disney World (Fla.) |
    Imaginary (Philosophy)
Classification: LCC E169.12 .G868 2023 | DDC 306.40973—dc23/eng/20220615
LC record available at https://lccn.loc.gov/2022008510

A British Cataloging-in-Publication record for this book is available from the British Library.

References to internet websites (URLs) were accurate at the time of writing. Neither the
author nor Rutgers University Press is responsible for URLs that may have expired or
changed since the manuscript was prepared.

☉ The paper used in this publication meets the requirements of the American National
Standard for Information Sciences—Permanence of Paper for Printed Library Materials,
ANSI Z39.48-1992.

www.rutgersuniversitypress.org

Manufactured in the United States of America

For Dottie and Penny, who never cease to inspire, surprise, and thrill me. Every day with you is better than any day without you.

Contents

The American Historical
Imaginary

Introduction

• •

This book has its genesis in two seemingly disparate sources—a fistfight I once narrowly avoided being a part of, and Walter Benjamin's often-quoted essay "On the Concept of History."

The near fight occurred as a result of anger both toward and in defense of the popularity of T-shirts from the (intentionally provocative) brand Dixie Outfitters among students of my high school. Dixie Outfitters is a clothing brand that traffics primarily in apparel adorned with the infamous Confederate battle flag. That symbol of white supremacy has become less mainstream in recent years—it was removed from the South Carolina statehouse in 2015 following the mass shooting at Mother Emmanuel Church in Charleston and from the Mississippi state flag in 2020 following the national uprisings triggered by the killing of George Floyd. In spite of this, the Confederate flag remains entrenched as a symbol in southern states to this day. In 2002, when I was a high school freshman, it adorned countless T-shirts in the halls of my South Carolina high school, most of which were manufactured by Dixie Outfitters. Some shirts simply associated the flag with a pleasant element of "southern" life—one design I saw often was an illustration of Labrador retriever puppies snuggling in a basket that was draped with the Confederate flag. Others were baldly racist hate speech; I vividly recall one that depicted enslaved people picking cotton under a banner that read, "I wish I was in Dixie" and another that showed the Confederate flag flying atop the South Carolina statehouse under the words "I have a dream."

In spite of protests led by Black students, the administration refused to ban these shirts from school property for a considerable time, during which tension steadily rose between students who wore Dixie Outfitters apparel and students who believed the brand should be banned from campus. As that tension approached its boiling point, I needled another student on my bus ride home about her Dixie Outfitters shirt—one that showed various flags of the Confederacy accompanied by the words "These colors don't run—Never have. Never will." This statement, I pointed out to the wearer, was not correct.

She angrily dismissed me, maintaining the shirt was accurate.

It could not be, I argued. The Confederacy had lost the Civil War. The colors had retreated on multiple occasions.

No, she again insisted, with increased intensity. These colors did not run.

All right, I conceded, feeling pleased as a way to further antagonize this opponent came to my mind. The colors did not run. Flags were not capable of voluntary movement. The people *carrying* the colors had run.

This brought her to her feet. I was wrong. And I needed to take back what I had said immediately, or she would deliver justice for those I had besmirched with my words via violence.

Keenly aware both of the certainty of my coming out the loser in such a confrontation and of how unsettlingly long bus fights tended to last, I backed down, offering the compromise that I would say no more about it. She accepted, and we remained hostile strangers from that day forward. Not long after, Dixie Outfitters shirts were banned from campus. The brand's storefront in my hometown remains open, and the shirts on its website still run the gamut from the "Dixie Baby" line of Confederate puppies and mama hens to slogans such as "I support LGBT—Liberty, Guns, Bible, Trump" and even a "School Protest" shirt that reads, "You can make me change my shirt, but I'll never change my mind."

Years later, in my graduate studies, I encountered the work of Walter Benjamin, a renowned twentieth-century philosopher and one of the foundational thinkers of the academic field of cultural studies. I did not immediately connect his posthumously published work "Theses on the Philosophy of History," to that now long-ago bus ride. But eventually one of that work's most frequently quoted passages led me to reexamine the Dixie Outfitters conflict. Benjamin writes, "To articulate the past historically does not mean to recognize it 'the way it really was.' It means to seize hold of a memory as it flashes up at a moment of danger" (255). What I now find interesting about that particular bus ride is not that my own blithe commitment to matching provocation with provocation blinded me to my opponent's intensity of feeling until she made an explicit threat of violence. Instead, it is that she held such commitment to a "history" that she undoubtedly knew to be untrue. Why did a "no surrender" version of the Confederacy exist in her mind when (in spite of our school's academic shortcomings) she had certainly been taught the same history I had? And since inescapable evidence abounded that she was in no way an anomaly, the question was not truly about her but about our shared culture—why do "debunked" histories persist in our shared cultural imagination? As this book will show, certain moments of cultural trauma in American history "flash up" at us in mass culture again and again. Sometimes we (the "we" here being those who seek a more just world and a true reckoning with the past's wrongs) seize hold of it, but more often it slips through our fingers. This, too, is something Benjamin recognized. In the same paragraph, he continues, "In every era the attempt must be made anew to wrest tradition away from a conformism that is about to over-power it.... Only that historian will have the gift of fanning the spark of hope in the past who is firmly convinced that *even the dead* will not be safe from the enemy if he wins" (255; emphasis in original).

I believe that the kind of historical knowledge Benjamin calls upon us to fight for is created not in the work of traditional history but in the historical imaginary as I am seeking to define it: a socially constructed understanding of the past formed through public discourse and representations, including those mobilized for entertainment, education, and politics. The historical imaginary is formed at a point of intersection between what has been established through the work of historians, and what has been represented in mass culture. It is shaped by fictionalized accounts of history, what is taught in school, popular political discourse, and spaces of cultural memory—all of which are influential in shaping what we "know" about the past. Unlike history, however, the historical imaginary is not required to root its claims in reliable sources to gain credibility, and so at any moment it may or may not be reflective of what actually occurred. While history may need to reconfigure its understanding of past events based on newly uncovered evidence or competing interpretations, the historical imaginary tends to withstand such revelations—as is apparent in the persistent myths around America's Founding Fathers, the first Thanksgiving, or countless other counterfactual histories that remain entrenched in the American cultural imagination.

The historical imaginary is frequently contested and renegotiated; however, it is inextricably intertwined with dominant ideologies and generally serves to rationalize and reinforce popular conceptions of national identity. This is not to say that every member of a given society is equally invested in the narratives of the historical imaginary. As Gary Edgerton writes in "Ken Burns's America," "Multiple renditions of the past can and do simultaneously coexist. On the other hand, not every version of history is permitted access to the country's airwaves" (50). Edgerton's mention of mass media resources is useful in understanding how the historical imaginary is constructed; without the broadly shared experiences made possible by mass media technologies—exposure to the same interpretations of the past on-screen, in textbooks, and in political discourse—a national historical imaginary could not exist.

However, rather than conceive of multiple, competing historical imaginaries, I believe it is more useful to understand the historical imaginary as functioning in terms of Antonio Gramsci's theorization of hegemony. Like hegemonic capitalism as defined by Gramsci, the historical imaginary has "accentuated the fragmentation and the divisions in the concrete whole formed by human beings, precisely in order to reinforce consensus and to legitimate itself" (Fernández Buey 107). In *Language and Hegemony in Gramsci*, Peter Ives identifies one of the main themes of hegemony as the "expansion of the definition of politics from activities of government and operations of state power to questions of how people come to understand the world" (70–71), and it is precisely this theme that illustrates the importance of examining the historical imaginary and the way in which it functions. This conception of the historical imaginary preserves space for subaltern understanding of past events that challenge dominant narratives without undercutting them. While we may not all subscribe to the ideologies mobilized by the historical imaginary, and there are many individuals who recognize the convenient fictions bound up within it for what they are, we all live with the repercussions of the world which shapes it and which it shapes in return. The rewriting of American history to reify hegemonic values is not a new phenomenon. However, it is an increasingly widespread and entrenched one. Consequences may be seen from the way the teaching of history is politicized, as in laws banning "critical race theory" in classrooms and controversy concerning the AP U.S. History Exam, to increasingly heated political discourse on who may be included in the category of "American."

The historical imaginary plays an outsize role in shaping the teaching of history in American schools compared with actual methods and findings of historians. One space in which this is visible is in the ongoing spectacle of the educational standards set by the Texas State Board of Education, whose curriculum choices have received increased media scrutiny in the last ten years. As detailed by Jonna Perrillo in "Once Again, Texas's Board of Education Exposed How Poorly We Teach History," conservative activist groups have used the educational standards set by the Texas State Board of Education as a means of disseminating counterfactual narratives of the past in the classroom since the Cold War, and "the board enthusiastically accepted the task. It repeatedly mandated the censorship or diminishment in history textbooks of, among other things, labor unions, Social Security, the United Nations, racial integration and the Supreme Court." At the same time, "it compelled the inclusion of 'the Christian tradition,' the free market and conservative heroes Joseph McCarthy, Herbert Hoover, Douglas MacArthur and Chiang Kai-shek." Texas continues to drive the framework adopted by most major textbook publishers; because one-tenth of American public school students live in Texas, publishers are unwilling to counter the state board's standards and risk rendering a textbook unusable there.

Debates around what to include and what to exclude, based not on histori-cal fact but on the narrative that supports a given view of national identity, are in no way limited to Texas. In 2014, when the AP U.S. History curriculum added standards that "address[ed] the conflicts between Native American and European settlers" and material that covered the contemporary "rise of social conservatism and the battles over issues such as abortion, as well as the fight against terrorism after the attacks of September 11, 2001," there was national outcry and pushback from conservatives, particularly in Colorado. The Jeffer-son County School District in Colorado appointed a committee to review the curriculum with the goal of ensuring classes "present the positive aspects of the United States and its heritage, and promote citizenship, patriotism, essen-tials and benefits of the free enterprise system." One parent, speaking in sup-port of that action, said she distrusted the new curriculum because it was "reviewed by college professors, and college professors are, by and large, on the left. . . . American exceptionalism is something our kids need to believe in" (Karen Tumulty and Lyndsey Layton). A few weeks later, the College Board revised the standards, capitulating to the demands of conservative ideol-ogy by instructing that teachers should emphasize the "Founding Documents, WWII, key leaders in the civil rights movement, and other topics" and that "teachers should help students understand that the statements in the frame-work represent common perspectives in college survey courses that merit famil-iarity, discussion, and debate. The AP Exam questions do not require students to agree with the statements" (Canedo).

It is almost impossible at this point to discuss the role of counterfactuality and distortions of both past and present realities in American discourse with-out acknowledging the impact of the presidency of Donald Trump. Indeed, the process of writing this book can be mapped along the timeline of Trump's presidency. One of my first public discussions of this theorization of the his-torical imaginary occurred the same week that Kellyanne Conway infa-mously informed Chuck Todd on *Meet the Press* that statements made on behalf of the president that had been labeled as falsehoods were simply "alternative facts" (Bradner). As I complete this book, Trump is once again a private citizen, but his legacy persists—not least because, largely swayed by his rhetoric, a majority of Republican voters maintain that the 2020 election was invalid (Easley). Throughout his presidency, Donald Trump was heavily invested in maintaining certain versions of American history. He attacked opponents on social media who advocated for the removal of Confederate memorials, even threatening to veto any bill that included provisions for renaming military bases named in honor of Confederate leaders (Scott). One of his final acts in office was to release the "1776 Report." The report, written without input from any historians, "offered a framework for a 'patriotic edu-cation.'" As described by Robyn Autry, the "1776 Report" "aligns progressive

politics with fascism, warns of communists masquerading as college professors and traces the origins of identity-based social movements to the pro-
slavery arguments of white supremacists like John C. Calhoun." There is no
denying that Trump's engagements with American history were consistently
far more invested in the historical imaginary than the actual past.

However, the role of the historical imaginary in American culture predates
Donald Trump's rise in politics and will persist long after his influence is
gone. The examples just described, as well as my own high school's challenge
in grappling with what Confederate history represents, demonstrate the
intensity of passionate resistance that is often inflamed when counterfactual
narratives of the historical imaginary face challenges based on the methods
and criteria of traditional history. This is not to say that such challenges are
inconsequential—indeed, they remain of vital importance, and the tenacity of
those committed to defending counterfactual histories in the name of ideological convenience must be met with equal tenacity by educators, activists,
and individuals committed to an honest national reckoning with the events of
the past. However, that door will be made easier to open if we can find new
ways to narrativize the past within the historical imaginary; shifting understandings of what the past means in the realm of imagination, play, and
entertainment may provide a fruitful way of challenging those narratives
before they calcify into ideology.

In *Weimar Cinema and After,* Thomas Elsaesser uses the term "historical
imaginary" to describe a "kind of slippage between cinematic representation
and a nation's history" (4). Jerome de Groot also mobilizes the concept of the
historical imaginary in *Consuming History,* in which he writes that through
the historical imaginary, history is bound up with "nationhood, nostalgia, com-
modity, revelation and knowledge . . . it is at once a deferred, distanced discourse and simultaneously something that the individual could literally at times
hold in their hand, change in their own way, or experience in a variety of mediums" (4). The historical imaginary's connection to history is necessarily slippery; it may have been best articulated in the film *The Man Who Shot Liberty
Valance* (1962) by a reporter who explains rejecting the opportunity to correct
a widely held falsehood by saying, "This is the West, sir. When the legend
becomes fact, print the legend." In such a formulation, rigorous historical methods are not irrelevant, but they rapidly lose ground to knowledge of the past
based in a sense of emotional truth or fidelity to a hegemonically determined
national identity. As de Groot points out, "In the contemporary Anglophone
world, the ways in which individuals encounter time, the past, 'history,' and
memory mostly fall outside an academic or professional framework" (7);
in order to examine social understandings of history, we must take those encounters seriously. The construction of the historical imaginary is one of the "pro-
cesses by which meaning is attached to the past" (Carlsten and McGarry 1); it

results from a shared negotiation of what we are willing to accept as the implications of our history and therefore is central to understanding how we come to "know," and know how to feel about, the past.

The historical imaginary informs how we feel about history as well as what we believe occurred in the past, and recent works that examine the potential uses of mass culture depictions of the past have frequently examined film and television's potential to elicit affective engagement from viewers. Marnie Hughes-Warrington describes historical films as "sites of relation" (6), where understandings of history are formed, set forth, and either accepted or contested. For Hughes-Warrington, it is important to see the relationship between filmmakers and viewers as dynamic; she argues that neither group consistently dominates the other. Similarly, in *Pastiche*, Richard Dyer explores how cinema elicits an emotional connection to the past through styles of filmmaking, offering another means of examining representations of the past without foregrounding questions of accuracy. Dyer rejects the negative connotations and critiques of postmodernism typically associated with the term "pastiche"; instead, he writes that "[pastiche] can at its best, allow us to feel our connection to the affective frameworks, the structures of feeling, past and present, that we inherit and pass on. That is to say, *it can enable us to know ourselves affectively as historical beings*" (180; emphasis added).

The possibility of mass culture sites functioning as a locations of meaningful encounters with history is examined by Alison Landsberg in *Engaging the Past: Mass Culture and the Production of Historical Knowledge*. Landsberg argues that mass-mediated encounters with historical events can result in serious engagements with the past that are primarily affective but not aimed at producing identification. When well mobilized, they have the potential to foster historical consciousness by simultaneously engaging the viewer emotionally and stymieing straightforward identification, thus encouraging the viewer to consider the gap between their own experience and the experiences of different historical moments. Not all (or even most) depictions of the past create the engagement Landsberg argues is politically useful. In discussing film, she points to those "that foreground mediation, that produce epistemological uncertainty through the layering of different types of footage, and that in a range of ways prevent us from losing ourselves in the illusion" (59) as the most effective vehicles for this experience. By forcing viewers to remain aware of their distance from the past and the mediation of their experience of it, encounters with the past that occur through film, television, or digital media may help form historical consciousness. The historical imaginary is ineluctably bound up with affective relations to history, which tend to set the limits for what kinds of understandings are tolerable within it; in other words, what we "know" about the past is inextricable from how we feel (or want to feel) about it.

The historical imaginary is the way we as a society have come to envision our shared history, and it is simultaneously susceptible to reshaping by shifting cultural values or highly influential interventions, and resistant to change through traditional historical methods. As in Charles Taylor's description of social imaginaries, the historical imaginary is "common understanding that makes possible common practices and a widely shared sense of legitimacy" (23). It is its ubiquity and the highly recognizable nature of its discourses, rather than archival evidence, that rationalizes the narratives of the historical imaginary. Like the national symbolic described by Lauren Berlant, the historical imaginary works "through images, narratives, monuments, and sites that circulate through personal/collective consciousness" (5). However, the function of the national symbolic is to form individuals within a nation into political subjects; the national symbolic's shaping of what it means to be a citizen "not only affects profoundly the citizen's subjective experience of his/her political rights, but also of civil life, private life, the life of the body itself" (20). The historical imaginary, by contrast, is not directly enmeshed with regulatory categories such as citizenship. Its inclusions and exclusions have political implications, and it is frequently deployed in political rhetoric, but it is primarily a space of social relation. Unlike the national symbolic, which uses the idea of patriotism to disguise its political implications, the historical imaginary attempts to use the supposed impartiality of history as an alibi to obscure any political investments.

American national identity has long been bound up with an understanding of the past that is influenced more by a drive to rationalize mainstream values and practices than by a rigorous look at the historical record. In *The Birth of a Nation*, Robert Lang describes one of the foremost examples of this phenomenon—the way the American Civil War is understood—and how rapidly mythology overcame fact on that subject. Lang writes, "The process of turning the bloody, traumatic reality into a Victorian melodrama began shortly after the fighting ceased. For Southerners and Northerners alike, it was a psychological necessity to make a legend out of the chaos and contradiction of the experience" (3). While the Civil War and the attendant horrors that both predated it (slavery) and emerged as consequences of it (particularly segregation, Jim Crow, and lynching) remain the most prominent instances of American trauma eased by melodramatic rescripting, they do not represent an isolated instance. The historical imaginary continuously works and reworks moments of national trauma that continue to "flash up" at us, seeking to defend the boundaries of a hegemonic national self-understanding that rejects its complicity in past injustices and horrors.

This book examines the functioning of the historical imaginary through mass cultural engagements with the past that use the question, "What if . . . ?" as their entry point into the past, rather than maintaining fidelity to historical accuracy. I have chosen a variety of mass culture narratives that depict the past in ways that the consumer is meant to understand as selectively inaccurate. These come from unscripted television, scripted television, the world's most popular theme park, and film. In choosing a variety of media forms, I am attempting to replicate the working of the historical imaginary. As the historical imaginary constantly traverses such boundaries in its formation, its analysis demands an interdisciplinary approach. That the selection of case studies here may seem eclectic is largely due to the impossibility of its being comprehensive— the historical imaginary inflects every depiction of the past in mass culture, and, as I have sought to demonstrate so far, the contested narratives of America's past profoundly impact the nation's present discourse.

Each of the sites I have chosen to analyze foregrounds some clear departure from the expectation of "historical accuracy" but also purports to provide some form of worthwhile insight into America's past. I have chosen these narratives in part because the ways in which they flag themselves as "play" or "entertainment" elide the impacts they have on cultural imaginings and understandings of the past. They are also of particular use because they are engagements of the historical imaginary with elements of American culture and identity that are most strongly contested at this time. In the cases studies I have selected, issues of race as well as questions of masculinity are particularly foregrounded. Conflicts around these identity categories have always been foundational to American national identity, but in the current moment they have largely shifted from the subtext to the text of national discourse. These sites are not afterthoughts to the formation of historical understanding in American culture—spaces of imaginative engagement with the past provide some of the clearest distillations of how we have come to understand America's past. It is in these imaginative spaces that important moments from our past "flash up" over and over, affording that opportunity to seize hold of them. At these sites of imaginative engagement, the most fraught moments of America's past are worked and reworked at the level of cultural imagination, often without regard for history.

The first chapter, "The History Channel's Reality Competitions," examines the relationship between narratives of material history and masculinity through competition programs produced for History (still popularly referred to by its former name, The History Channel). These series depict pedagogical authority over history as lying in mastery of skill sets imagined to be the unique legacy of white masculinity, and the past as a space where fragile masculinity can be reaffirmed. While concerns of gender are frequently elided in the historical imaginary, which has a tendency to insist on an undifferentiated citizen as the subject of its address, the competition programs of History provide an opportunity for a clear distillation of hegemonic strategies in the historical imaginary for resisting any shifts in understanding of what hegemonic masculinity signifies.

The second chapter, "Time Travel Television Series," examines four television series that premiered in 2016, all of which take up the question of whether the past "should" be changed, and involve either an educator or a historian (or both) who journeys to significant moments of American national trauma and must decide whether or not to intercede in the events of history. These series articulate the historical imaginary's understanding of what a historian can and should do, and their prescription is intensely limiting. By examining these shows, I demonstrate how the historical imaginary seeks to close its narratives off from new scrutiny and vilifies contemporary historians who seek to "rewrite history."

The third chapter, "American History in Walt Disney World's Magic Kingdom," examines how the American history–themed sections of the world's most popular theme park naturalize the ideology of the American historical imaginary through the narratives visitors construct for themselves by navigating the physical space of the park. Through a skillful interweaving of melodrama and nostalgia, the Magic Kingdom constructs the past as a space that always leads to a necessary happy ending—a foundational tenet of the historical imaginary, which acknowledges history's wrongs only as necessary stepping-stones toward a triumphant present.

The fourth chapter, "The European Legacy and American Future in Walt Disney World's Magic Kingdom," continues the examination of the Magic Kingdom through the sections of the park that are themed around the histories of Europe and European imperialism, as well as an imagined future. These spaces provide an opportunity to examine how the American historical imaginary understands itself as the heir to European imperialism, a facet of American history rarely made explicit in mass culture, and its relation to potential utopian futures. By devoting two chapters to the Magic Kingdom here, I recognize that there may be a perception that Disney occupies an outsize space in this book. However, there is no question that the Disney Corporation does in fact occupy an outsize role in American mass media through its continuous expansions and acquisitions. While much outstanding scholarship has been produced on Disney's films, the space of the parks has received much less consideration. The theme parks represent those elements of the corporation's ideology that it considers to be most stable; films and television series may be responsive to trends, since more are constantly being made, but a theme park attraction is meant to remain in place, with minimal if any change, for decades. This is why I believe the clearest articulation of the Disney Corporation's impact on the historical imaginary can be made legible through examination of its most popular theme park, and that it is worthwhile to analyze the entire space.

The fifth chapter, "Quentin Tarantino's Alternate Histories," examines three films in which writer-director Quentin Tarantino dramatically ruptures the expected narrative of history in order to challenge widely held conceptions of the past. These films insist to the viewer that history is not inert, and they potentially provide new ways of thinking about both the events of the past and these events' reverberations in the present moment.

Understanding and meaningfully engaging with the historical imaginary provides a useful inroad to understanding the role of history in American culture. The historical imaginary, mass culture, and history exist in often uneasy or even fraught constellation with one another in American culture. This book seeks to make the functions of this dynamic clear, because understanding the historical imaginary provides a useful inroad to making sense of the role our conception of the past plays in American culture. Through the following chapters, this book provides an overview both of the strategies the historical imaginary deploys in defending its narratives of the past in spite of the interventions of historians over the years and of potential strategies to, in the terms of Walter Benjamin, perhaps finally seize control of the narratives of our history the next time they inevitably flash up at us.

1

The History Channel's
Reality Competitions

●●●●●●●●●●●●●●●●●●●●●

Since it began airing in 1995, The History Channel has maintained strong rat-
ings and been home to a number of popular programs that claim to provide
useful knowledge about the past, in spite of the fact that its programming has
been subject to widespread and continuous mockery in popular culture. In the
channel's early years, its heavy reliance on documentaries and series focused on
World War II—often as much as twelve hours a day—led to it being nicknamed
"The Hitler Channel," a designation that had previously been assigned to The
History Channel's originator, A&E (Schone). The channel's early years were
dominated by typical forms of "great man" history, particularly American military history. This focus shaped its presentation of the past as being the near-
exclusive purview of white men, both because discriminatory practices barred
all others from midcentury military leadership and because of programming
choices that valorized rather than critiqued the American past. In "The History Channel and the Challenge of Historical Programming" (2000), Brian
Taves notes that at the time he was writing, The History Channel largely relied
on preexisting, cheaply available documentaries from the United States and
United Kingdom to fill airtime, and the original, reenactment-based films
and series it produced tended, largely due to budget constraints, to be "second-
rate work" (15). However, Taves lauded The History Channel for refusing to
delve into sensationalized and dubious programs like those of other "documentary" cable channels, noting that "Discovery and TLC have dived unashamedly
into programming on aliens and ufo's—a field where The History Channel has,

for the most part, not followed.... [The History Channel] generally refuses to shift toward sensationalized or trivial subject matter" (14). Taves's hope was that The History Channel would continue and grow stronger in that vein, providing a channel for a limited but steady audience interested in traditional documentary programs covering well-researched history.

More recently, the channel's trajectory has changed so dramatically that Taves's generous assessment has become unfortunately comical in hindsight. In 2008, The History Channel changed its name to History; around the same time, it dramatically shifted its primary programming to reality shows and speculative and conspiracy theory–based series. The channel's website lists 208 past and current programs, only 67 of which are nonfiction documentaries in the traditional sense. The informative programs lauded by Taves have since been outnumbered by reality shows, of which the site lists 73. History's program offerings are rounded out by fictional programs, series focused on speculative "investigations," and a handful of game shows and comedy programs. Despite this, it continues marketing itself as a serious source of knowledge. The channel's official website includes a "This Day in History" feature and publishes numerous well-researched articles such as "5 Vice Presidential Candidates Who Made History" and "How the 1968 Sanitation Workers' Strike Expanded the Civil Rights Struggle," all of which combine to connote reliability and authority. The channel simultaneously houses a number of contradictory impulses in understanding the past—unscripted "reality" programming, unchecked speculation set free from any expectations of supporting evidence, and traditional documentary programs. As such, it is an ideal site for examining the dynamic between the historical imaginary, mass media, and history in conceptualizing America's past at an intersection that lays claim to both education and entertainment.

The History network has become most notorious for its speculative series, particularly *Ancient Aliens*. It has produced fifteen seasons of the show since 2010; in each episode, individuals presented as experts posit the behind-the-scenes influence of aliens in almost every human endeavor across time. The series' most recognizable aspect is its co–executive producer and star, Giorgio A. Tsoukalos, who is described on History's website as "a hybrid of Carl Sagan and Indiana Jones" and has been popularized in meme form via a screenshot from the show showing him midsentence, hands raised in an emphatic gesture, and captioned with mocking invented quotes like, "I'm not saying it was aliens ... but it was aliens" and "I don't know. Therefore aliens" (Kurutz). In addition to online mockery, History's speculative series have faced an endless stream of critique from scientific and academic communities. A typical example is the *Smithsonian Magazine*'s article "The Idiocy, Fabrications, and Lies of Ancient Aliens," in which the series is described as "some of the most noxious sludge in television's chum bucket" (Black). In spite of all this, speculative programs continue to make up a significant portion of History's output; 48 of the 208 shows listed on the channel's website are speculative, offering either aliens, supernatural forces, or unsubstantiated "new evidence" as means of explaining the past and present.

While a newfound fixation on alien intervention in humanity's past is a departure from continuous World War II documentaries, these shows serve the interests of the same target audience: white American men. Individuals invested in UFO conspiracy theories are overwhelmingly white, particularly white men, and the feats of ancient human architecture commonly pointed to as proof of alien assistance overwhelmingly originate in the global south. In an excerpt from his book published on the *Today* website, humorist Larry Wilmore questioned why Black people have seemingly been excluded from UFO sightings. He points to an instance of a UFO sighting shared by "99.9 perfect of the residents" of a small community in 1987. However, Wilmore notes that what most interested him was "the .1 percent that didn't see the UFO. That .1 percent was named Clerow Mims: the only black resident of the city. How come brothas don't see UFOs? I have asked this question for the last thirty years and have yet to stumble upon any satisfactory answer." As described more seriously by Julien Benoit, white interest in extraterrestrial intervention in human history is rooted in discrimination. He writes it is "so hard for some to acknowledge that ancient non-European civilizations like the Aztecs, people from Easter Island, ancient Egyptians or Bantu-speakers from southern African could create intricate structures" because of "profound racism and a feeling of white superiority that emanates from the rotting corpse of colonialism." As the History channel has shifted away from military history, it has maintained a particular focus on conceptions of white masculinity. This is particularly apparent in the unscripted reality shows that dominate the channel's current lineup.

In spite of the popular perception of History as being a network dominated by UFO conspiracists, reality series significantly outnumber speculative programming in the channel's list of offerings—there are more than one and a half times as many reality programs on History's website as there are speculative series. The channel has even released more reality shows than documentary programs: seventy-three reality shows to sixty-seven documentaries and documentary series. History's reality programs focus almost exclusively on the careers, skills, or interests of the white men they overwhelmingly feature. Taken as a whole, these series use a variety of strategies in an attempt to balance conflicting idealized forms of masculinity. History's reality programs must negotiate hegemonic masculinity's impulses to idealize the apparently conflicting values of physical domination/violence and self-control/rationality. The former tends to be demonstrated through the image of rugged, working-class men in dangerous professions (e.g., *Swamp People*, *Mountain Men*, and *Ice Road Truckers*), while the latter is achieved with depictions of men with highly specialized skill sets, particularly those connected to the past (e.g., *Pawn Stars*, *American Pickers*, and *American Restoration*). All position the past as a moment of superior masculinity and emphasize the edifying nature of thriving in predigital circumstances. Richard Dyer describes the tension between these poles of masculinity in *White*, writing "the white insistence on spirit, on a transcendent relation to the body, has also led to a view that perhaps non-whites have better bodies, run faster," but that "the possibility of white bodily inferiority falls heavily on the shoulders of those white men who are not at the top of the spirit pile" (147). In its various reality programs, History provides a portrayal of masculinity that attempts to reaffirm the association between white masculinity and physical prowess and/or the association between white masculinity and intellectual authority demonstrated through the mastery of special skills.

None of History's reality programs follow the format that first popularized the idea of understanding the past through reality television, which involved placing everyday people in material circumstances that mimicked living conditions of the past. This genre of historically invested reality television, particularly the programs *Frontier House*, *Colonial House*, and *Texas Ranch House*, are examined by Alison Landsberg in *Engaging the Past: Mass Culture and the Production of Historical Knowledge*. Landsberg argues that "reenactment-based reality history TV shows" can produce useful knowledge about the past "when a delicate balance is maintained between drawing individuals into specific scenarios/crises/issues of the past in an affective, palpable way and yet also relentlessly reminding them of their distance and difference from the past" (118). History's reality programs, by contrast, eschew the portrayal of the past as distant in favor of its being portrayed as continuous. The Louisiana-based alligator hunters of *Swamp People*, for example, are contemporary individuals living in the modern world—it is their connection to a certain white, rural, physically challenging, and dangerous form of masculinity that codes them as simultaneously being sufficiently representative of the past to qualify for a spot in History's lineup.

This chapter examines two of History's most successful reality programs, *Forged in Fire* (2015–present) and *Alone* (2015–present). These series provide clear and useful insights into how elements of the past are selectively chosen and integrated into the historical imaginary to shape an understanding of contemporary masculinity that balances the tension between the two forms of masculinity described here and renders a clear vision of the channel's idealized male subject. Both series are competition reality shows—participants vie with one another for a cash prize either in each episode (*Forged in Fire*) or across the season (*Alone*). This element is an important aspect of their appeal, in that they are an implicit pitch for the accessibility of the series' undertakings. Recent seasons of both have included contestants describing how their own experiences watching the series inspired them to either learn the skills they needed to compete or influenced their strategies upon being selected for the show. Many of History's reality programs that only lasted one or two seasons committed completely to one of those two poles of masculinity—series like *Knight Fight* and *Kings of Pain* focused entirely on physical prowess, while a program like *Top Shot* was almost entirely centered on skills in weaponry. But while *Forged in Fire* and *Alone* assert a version of masculinity as defined by rugged individualism and skills in weaponry, they also position these skills as both available and useful in everyday life; provide viewers with a sense of shared expertise with the series' participants and judges; and model an idealized white, male, purportedly historical subject on whom viewers are encouraged to pattern themselves.

Forged in Fire

In 2017, a massive fire raged through downtown Cohoes, New York. While there were no serious injuries, homes were damaged or even destroyed, and as many as twenty-eight people were displaced. Felony charges of arson and reckless endangerment were filed against John Gomes, a plumber and father of two. However, this was no ordinary arson case. The fire was set unintentionally (the charges reflected perceived recklessness), and Gomes apparently set the blaze, in the words of Cohoes mayor Shawn Morse, "trying to bend metal and make a hammer or something." Gomes had been watching the History series *Forged in Fire* and had been inspired to try his hand at creating his own blacksmith forge at home (Fortin). He was sentenced to a year in jail, with terms that did not require him to pay the more than $600,000 he owed in restitution (Hughes). In spite of Gomes's (and the community of Cohoes's) misfortune, *Forged in Fire* remains a popular series, and many competitors appearing on the series describe taking up blacksmithing as a hobby after seeing the show.

Forged in Fire is History's most prolific reality competition program. Each episode features a blacksmithing tournament in which contestants create bladed weapons. These are then put to a variety of durability and use tests by the series' judges. The series has aired eight seasons since 2015 and has largely adhered to the same formula throughout its run, with minimal variation for "special" episodes. Most episodes begin with the introduction of four "bladesmiths," who are then tasked with salvaging metal from a given object (e.g., a car, a pinball machine, nautical equipment, elevator cables) to create a blade in a certain style or matching certain dimensions. At the end of the round their blades are critiqued by the judges, and one competitor is eliminated. The remaining three then participate in a second timed round in which they must correct whatever issues with their blades have been pointed out by the judges as well as create handles for their blades. After this round, the three blades are tested by the judges for durability and sharpness. Another contestant is eliminated based on these tests, and the remaining two contestants return to their "home forges" for five days to re-create an assigned sword or bladed weapon the series has deemed to have historical significance. These weapons are then put through a similar round of tests as the previous blades, and the winner is awarded $10,000.

The cast of *Forged in Fire* has remained largely consistent throughout its run. The original host, Wil Willis, left the series after season 7 and was replaced by Grady Powell. Both men are former members of the military; Willis served as both an Army Ranger and air force pararescueman, while Powell was a U.S. Army Green Beret and senior detachment weapons sergeant. Both segued their military service into careers in military-themed reality television before joining *Forged in Fire*. Willis appeared as himself in series such as *Rescue Warriors* (2005), *Special Ops Mission* (2009), and *Triggers: Weapons That Changed the World* (2011) prior to hosting *Forged in Fire*; Powell was a cast member of the reality series *Stars Earn Stripes* (2012), *Ultimate Survival Alaska* (2013–2015), *Dual Survival* (2010–2016), and *American Grit* (2016–2017). Thus, even though *Forged in Fire* is not an explicitly military-themed series, its host has always been someone with a preestablished public persona as a military serviceman, remaining consistent with History's interests prior to its turn toward speculative/reality programming. As host, Willis or Powell describes the specific challenges and guidelines to the contestants, announce the individual eliminated from each round, and converse with the judges during rounds to ask questions about and comment on the contestants' choices. The host serves as audience stand-in during conversation with the judges; in one interview Willis described his role as making sure the conversation stays grounded and approachable for lay viewers. As he explained, "They'll start talking about the atoms in the metal and that's great, man. Just tell me what's happening" (Kryah).

The judging panel is typically made up of J. Neilson, David Baker, and Doug Mercaida. Only Neilson is presented as an expert in the style of blacksmith work the contestants participate in on the show. Neilson's cast biography on the History website leans heavily on language of rugged individualism in describing his work—in part it states that "forging blades professionally, out of his 'shop in the woods' in the endless mountains of northeastern Pennsylvania, has made J. an expert in 'sole authorship' blade-making, a total mastery of every element of weapon design and manufacture" (https://www.history .com). The weapons' aesthetic qualities are judged by David Baker. Prior to *Forged in Fire*, Baker's career largely centered on creating prop weapons for film and television productions, particularly the Spike TV series *Deadliest Warrior*. However, his cast biography creatively elides the inherently artificial nature of this undertaking and focuses instead on his purported historical expertise. Notably, the word "prop" is absent from his biography on History, and there is no discussion of the types of media he has worked for. Instead, Baker's biography describes him as "constantly challenging his scholarship of weaponry." It goes on to proclaim that he "has been called upon to make weapons that haven't been seen outside of museums in centuries" and that he "is the go-to guy for accurate replicas from samurai swords to submachine guns." Doug Mercaida is described in his History biography as "a highly skilled martial artist who has also studied fighting styles and techniques from around the world." His primary role in the show is testing the contestants' weapons in "combat" situations. His catchphrase on the series, pronounced approvingly whenever a blade passes a second-round use test, is "It will K.E.Al." While not addressed in the show, this is not a mispronunciation of "It will kill" but a phrasing developed by Mercaida to mean "keep everyone alive." Mercaida's website explains that this expression evolved from his belief that "it's not about how many you hurt, it's about how many you protect." That Mercaida typically announces a given weapon will "K.E.Al." after he has demonstrated its effectiveness at shredding an animal carcass or red-goo-spewing ballistics dummy is not acknowledged as a source of potential cognitive dissonance on the show or on Mercaida's website.

Contestants on *Forged in Fire* are overwhelmingly white men. Women rarely appear—in the series' eight seasons, only two episodes have seen a woman blade-smith triumph in the competition (Kelly Vermeer-Vella in season 3 and Rita Thurman in season 7), and in the first season there were no women contestants at all. Tim Healy, History's head of programming and development, argued this was because of a lack of interested participants. He recounted, "It was tricky getting women because it was tricky just finding enough men . . . it takes a lot of guts to do this because your skill is being put on display and it's not easy to lose." Contradictorily, in the same interview Healy also defended the lack of women as being an element of the show's integrity: "I don't want to shoehorn in female characters for the sake of having female characters. So what's really important to us as a brand is the level of authenticity. I think as a network we're constantly striving to be more diverse and to expand the range of our characters, but it really comes down to that authenticity" (O'Keefe). The discussion of authenticity is odd because it seems to imply that women smiths were available but somehow less "authentic" than men. The couching of this discussion of authenticity in History's "brand" indicates that the exclusion of women was a strategic choice driven by a desire to present an image of blacksmithing that reads to viewers as "historically accurate." The show is about contemporary smiths but also is highly committed to demonstrating that mastery of a skill set associated with historical masculinity bolsters contemporary manhood. The inclusion of women sharing in that skill set would make the discourse illegible. While men of color compete on the show somewhat more often than women do, in the majority of episodes there are no women present, and the only person of color on screen is Mercaida, who was born in the Philippines. However, unlike the other two judges and the contestants, he does not have expertise in

bladesmithing (aside from what information he has picked up from participating in the show over the seasons).

Healy's contradictory statements—that women were searched for but either
unavailable or lacking the "guts" to be willing to publicly compete, and that
women were available and willing but their inclusion would have been an inauthentic "shoehorn"—are reflective of the show's desire to depict its forges as a
haven of masculinity without being explicitly exclusionary. In interviews, the
judges are consistently quick to make claims about the show's inclusivity,
the diversity of its fans, and the wide availability of the endeavor of working
at the forge. In an effusive feature written for *Vice* by Eve Peyser, a journalist
who describes herself in the piece as falling in love with the show after stumbling upon it while staying in a hotel, David Baker recounts a fan who told
him, "My daughter, she asked for an anvil for her birthday. She's six." Doug
Mercaida notes, "I get far more messages from people who watch this show
with their daughters than their sons." He argues that the gender imbalance
in smithing is due to popular misunderstandings: "This has been a male-
dominated industry because they see the fire—the muscle. Even I thought
that's what every blacksmith was supposed to be. But when you understand
the science and are educated on how to do it, you realize anybody and everybody can do it." In spite of this, the day Peyser visited the set was like the vast
majority of episodes. Contestants were "all white men, from various parts of
rural America."

Forged in Fire is often lauded for the environment of positivity, support, and
sportsmanship that it fosters. Peyser's feature is titled "The Nicest Reality Show
on TV Is All about Deadly Weapons," and she is by no means alone in her
analysis. Kristy Puchko's review of the program for *Pajiba*, "*Forged in Fire* Is a
Charming Challenge to Toxic Masculinity," praises the series for "provid[ing]
a wide array of positive male role models, men who relish being masculine, yet
are happy to share their softer side." Puchko, like Peyser, discovered the series
while channel surfing in a hotel. However, she proclaims that she is disinter-
ested in the weaponry and forging, even that she finds the sometimes-gory
weapons tests off-putting. Instead, Puchko writes that she is "here for the men
who managed to be passionate and manly without being competition-crazy,
agro-dickheads." Contestants are never encouraged by judges to denigrate the
work of other participants; judges' critiques are almost always accompanied by
some kind of praise or sympathy; and in their voice-overs reflecting on their
defeats, eliminated contestants express their disappointment with equanimity
and good humor. While Puchko's review is playfully hyperbolic, she is correct
that the series is modeling a certain type of masculinity, and it is a different
one than is typically presented in reality television. Indeed, the reality show
with an ethos of competition most similar to *Forged in Fire* is one not typically
associated with masculinity at all: *The Great British Baking Show*. Much like

the description of *The Great British Baking Show* given in the *Los Angeles Time*, on *Forged in Fire*, "contestants never say things like 'I didn't come here to make friends.' There are no irritating product placements" (Blake). In both series, contestants support one another's endeavors, and freely admire each other's work. However, the cast of *The Great British Baking Show* consistently reflects both racial and gender diversity. *Forged in Fire* remains a space committed to exclusionary white masculinity.

The third episode of season 6 provides a particularly useful example of the show's engagement with both understandings of masculinity and the historical imaginary. While the series always ostensibly connects to history, both by virtue of the channel it airs on and in the selection of the weapon to re-create in the final round, this episode brings understandings of the past into each part of the episode by theming its competition around American presidents. The episode's contestants are typical for the show. First introduced is Dan Burlows, a metallurgical engineer from Kentucky with seventeen years of experience as a "part-time bladesmith." In his introductory segment, Burlows describes bladesmithing as "this perfect blend of art and science and skill," immediately highlighting the idea of masculinity being tied to mastery of specialized expertise. Next is John Sims, a "hobbyist bladesmith" of two years. Sims comments that he is a "quiet and softer spoken individual" and that "people tend to think that I'm an asshole. I'm really not." Sims does not include his experience or interest in forging in his introduction, instead focusing on how he tends to be misunderstood or negatively judged. His interest in bladesmithing gives him his "own little world," as well as something to connect with others about ("I'll talk to you for hours"); it provides a structure for his internal and external identity. (This may seem like a large claim to make for a contestant with two years' experience, but Sims was only twenty-one when he appeared on the show.) Andrew Smith is then introduced as a part-time bladesmith of ten years. Smith explains that after making his first blade he "geeked out" over knives and has been making them ever since. He proclaims that if he wins the $10,000 prize, "First thing I'm doing is getting some [chicken] wings. Second thing I'm doing, I don't know, maybe buy a kayak. Something like that." Smith laughs at this comment, clearly intending it lightheartedly, but he is still tapping in to the connection to typical masculinity in this intention of eating meat and investing in a hobby associated with physical skill and the outdoors. The final contestant is Josh Nikolaidis, who has been a part-time bladesmith for five years. He says he took up the hobby because when he was practicing survival skills, the store-bought knives "just turned out to be junk." He says that his friends would describe him "as the goofy redneck from down the road," and he endorses this description. Nikolaidis's introduction highlights another type of masculine endeavor that is of frequent interest on the History channel—survivalism—as well as the do-it-yourself ethos of rugged individualism.

With the contestants in place, Will Willis introduces the first round's challenge as being in honor of President Theodore Roosevelt. Willis then gives a brief rundown of Roosevelt's accomplishments that led to his being selected for this honor: "He was born sickly and weak, but he overcame adversity to win the Nobel Peace Prize, and he led the first United States volunteer calvary during the Spanish-American War, and his unit was known as the Rough Riders." Willis then unveils a Rough Riders bowie knife the contestants must replicate from a piece of W1 round stock, a form of steel popular in forging. The provided material allows contestants to forgo the typical challenge of repurposing forging material in exchange for having to meet more precise than usual standards in their replication of the Rough Rider bowie (Willis describes the standard they will be judged by as "exacting"). Further emphasizing the historical nature of the challenge, the written parameters are provided to contestants on scrolls—a means of message conveyance associated generally with the past but in no way connected to Roosevelt.

The historical description of Roosevelt provided here is accurate but also misleading, as it implicitly connects his Nobel Peace Prize with his physical abilities. Willis ties Roosevelt's winning the prize with his having overcome the physical limitations of being born "sickly and weak." In actuality, Roosevelt won the 1906 Nobel Peace Prize for his role in aiding negotiations around the end of the Russo-Japanese War that resulted in the signing of the Treaty of Portsmouth. Presumably that is something he would have been capable of even if he had not so fully overcome his debilitating childhood asthma; winning the Nobel Prize only required him to overcome being "sickly and weak" to the extent he needed to survive childhood and hold a political position. In spite of the way Willis lays out the information about Roosevelt, the Rough Riders predated his Nobel Peace Prize by eight years, and there was no direct connection between the two. Roosevelt's history with the Rough Riders is clearly the aspect of his past that the show is interested in, but it is notable that this other accomplishment is thrown into the middle of the narrative of Roosevelt's ascent from unhealthy child to calvary leader. It implies, as Mercaida does with his insistence on distinguishing "kill" from "K.E.Al.," a cause-and-effect relationship between effectively wielded bladed weapons and a peaceful, safe environment.

As contestants begin forging their blades, the judges quickly transition from discussing the particular difficulties of this challenge to the history of the Rough Riders. Mercaida notes that Baker is a frequent horseback rider and asks where he thinks the Rough Riders would have carried their blades. Baker explains the bowie would be on the left hip and a pistol would be on the right. It is difficult to conceive of a way that being a hobbyist equestrian provided Baker with that knowledge, but *Forged in Fire* never wavers from its ideological commitment to the idea that having competence in some skill or endeavor that was useful in the past conveys authority of historical knowledge to an individual. Ben Abbott, a two-time *Forged in Fire* winner substituting for J. Neilson, then adds, "I would also posit that it [the Rough Rider bowie] was a good choice for the Rough Riders because it's a very American knife." There is no elaboration to this comment; instead, the presumption that an American-designed and American-made weapon will best serve an American calvary unit is treated as self-evidently true.

Because of the unusually precise requirements of these bowie replicas, three of the contestants do not (in the show's terms) "make parameters." In instances where only one contestant does not make parameters, this is cause for immediate dismissal from competition. With three falling short, there is a "sudden death" round, where the three subpar blades are tested for durability by being set against an industrial nut and then hammered with a baton by Abbott. Smith's blade suffers the "catastrophic failure" of its tang snapping off. This means there is no way to attach a handle to the blade, and Smith is eliminated from competition. Smith's exit commentary, which plays over footage of him shaking hands with other contestants and walking out of the forge, displays the kind of emotionally secure sportsmanship that is typical of the show's eliminated contestants. "This did not go in my favor," Smith says, still smiling. He adds that when he gets home he is "probably gonna make a bowie knife out of W1, with the tang still on."

Discussion during the second round eschews the topic of Roosevelt or history in favor of focusing on the technical aspects of improving the blades and attaching the handles. In the judging round, the blades are first tested for durability. This is done by having Abbott repeatedly whack the sharp edge of the blades against moose antlers (a clear reference to "Bull Moose" Theodore Roosevelt, though no one comments on this) and then examine the blades for damage. The bowies are then given to Mercaida for the sharpness test. Mercaida explains that he will be testing to see if the blades maintained their edges during the previous test by using them to slice into a large fish that is hanging from the ceiling. Both of these tests are scored to up-tempo instrumental rock guitar and drums, and both make use of slow-motion camerawork. This is particularly true of Mercaida's tests, where at various times Mercaida's arm drawing back or following through, as well as chunks of fish and moisture flying through the air, are all shown in lingering slow motion. Because Sims' blade is the only one to take damage in the strength test, he is eliminated, leaving with the same equanimity that Smith showed, explaining, "I came here to prove to myself that I am working down the right path of my craftsmanship, and I believe I've proved that to myself under these conditions."

Next, Willis introduces the two remaining contestants to the "iconic weapon from history" they will be re-creating for the final round: George Washington's colichemarde. Willis then provides a history of the weapon and

Washington's fondness for it. This information is presented in voice-over as the viewer is shown a montage of period illustrations of the weapon and Washington, as well as footage of a reenactor in a swordfight:

> The colichemarde was a unique dueling sword that became popular during the late 17th century and was a favorite blade style of George Washington. The weapon had an extremely broad forte, which gave the blade ample parrying strength. However, the sword rapidly tapered to a thin point, allowing for precise thrusting and stabbing attacks. An avid sword collector, George Washington even had a colichemarde bladed small sword at his side while swearing in as America's first president. The weapon was such an iconic part of Washington's persona, one can even be spotted alongside the first president in this iconic 1824 John Trumbull painting [*General George Washington Resigning His Commission*].

While the use of Trumbull's painting as a famous depiction is atypical for the show, which typically favors a movie or video game appearance as the example to close Willis's explanatory montage (the *Assassin's Creed* video games have come up on multiple occasions), it is in keeping with the episode's stated to desire to pay particular homage to the presidents. Trumbull's painting brings an additional aura of historical accuracy and reverence to the depiction of Washington's weapon.

Provided with the parameters and released to their home forges, the contestants are accompanied home by camera crews that track their progress over five days of work. Here, the viewer is given a glimpse into the lives of the bladesmiths, and the show centers their individualism and do-it-yourself work ethic. Both contestants live in rural areas, and this is repeatedly emphasized visually throughout the segment covering this round. There are establishing shots of empty, grassy fields and blooming wildflowers, with no neighboring homes in sight. Both are shown working alone, with no sign of any other household members. As he begins work, Nikolaidis acknowledges, "It's definitely the most intricate sword I've ever made." He then adds, "But I'm confident that I can redneck engineer it" (this marks the third time Nikolaidis has self-identified as a redneck in the episode). Both contestants are depicted as struggling to complete the challenge. Nikolaidis has to start over after an entire day's work because he made his blade too thin, and Burlows loses time making repeated hour-long drives to the hardware store after he first runs out of propane and then suffers the misfortune of his grinder breaking. While they express some frustration, both take these setbacks in stride, voicing that there is nothing for them to do other than continue working.

Back at the forge, the finished blades are first subjected to "the kill test," where Mercaida uses each sword to slice and thrust into a pig carcass in order to test its lethality. Once again, rock music and liberal use of slow motion accompany Mercaida's attack. Both swords earn the designation of "it will K.E.Al." Baker then tests the strength of the blades with, in honor of George Washington, "the cherry wood chop." He swings the blades into and bends them against the hard wood to test their durability. Nikolaidis's blade succeeds, but Burlows's fails to return to its original shape after being bent against the wood. There are several moments of reaction before Baker addresses this. Willis and the other two judges are shown reacting and whispering among themselves. Abbott grimaces and almost doubles over in apparent sympathy, Mercaida appears to give a rueful laugh and headshake, while Willis leans back and winces like a high school football player with mixed feelings about seeing a friend taken down in an impressive tackle. Burlows is shown frowning and mouthing indecipherable words to someone offscreen. But he nods and quietly accepts both Baker's critique ("The heat treat on this blade has just failed") and compensatory praise ("I think you did a beautiful job constructing this weapon"). Mercaida then steps back in for the sharpness test, which is to be conducted by slashing and stabbing the blades into bags of colored sand hanging from the ceiling. This is shot almost entirely in slow motion, with lovingly shot sword swings and blue sand streaming dramatically through the air and creating a visually striking cloud of blue fog along the ground. However, due to the bend in Burlows's blade, Mercaida determines it is not safe to test, and Burlows is eliminated. In his departing voice-over, Burlows states, "Leaving this, I feel like I learned more than a lot of other times in my life, and I finished a better smith than I was before, and really that's the best I can hope for."

In his review of the series for the *Baltimore Sun*, Brandon Weigel describes the appeal of *Forged in Fire* as "a callback to our country's height as an industrial powerhouse, when red-blooded American men could make a good living using their hands, and so much of what we bought proudly said 'Made in the U.S.A.'" That this show appeals to this particular version of masculinity presumed to be best represented by America's past—one that is implicitly racial segregated and patriarchal—is unquestionably true. *Forged in Fire* offers a view of white masculinity, often narrativized as being "under attack" by so-called cancel culture or otherwise "in crisis," as redeemable by retreating to skills most associated with a past era before it became quite so brittle. The show models perseverance and humility as masculine values, but it also demonstrates deep-seated racial and gender bias in its understanding of who may be expected to embody them. Its engagement with the historical imaginary is through this particular narrative of white masculinity—one that demands both physical acumen and specialized skills. Most important, it posits that mastery of skills that were important to the "great men" of the past conveys their historical authority to those men seeking a similarly rarefied experience of the present.

FIGURE 1 Doug Mercaida uses a competitor's weapon to slash through colorful sandbags in slow motion. (Credit: Screenshot from *Forged in Fire*.)

Alone

The History series *Alone* received what was likely an unexpected endorsement on December 18, 2020. In a special live episode of the popular comedy podcast *How Did This Get Made?*, hosted over a video chat service and livestreamed to ticket holders with the appropriate link, actor-comedians Paul Scheer, Jason Mantzoukas, June Diane Rapheal, and Jessica St. Clair gathered to discuss the Netflix holiday movie *The Knight before Christmas*. The conceit of the podcast is the three hosts (Scheer, Mantzoukas, and Rapheal), often joined by a guest (St. Clair is the most popular and frequent of these), watch and then discuss a film that is so unusual, nonsensical, or simply terrible that its having been produced and released is inherently puzzling. The podcast appeals to a fairly broad audience. The cast and guests are popular with comedy fans; Scheer and Mantzoukas have strong backgrounds in improv comedy and a tendency to pop up in a wide variety of sitcoms and comedy movies, Rapheal is a core cast member of the Netflix series *Grace and Frankie*, among many other credits for comedic roles, and many prominent comedians have guested on the show. Fans of Hollywood, in addition to satisfying their curiosity about the films discussed, can enjoy that the working actors hosting the podcast offer a great deal of insider insight into the entertainment industry. General fans of popular culture may be engaged by the highly referential show, with its hosts often reminiscing about their experiences with movies like *Grease 2*, *Drop Dead Fred*, and the *Star Wars* franchise. All these factors have contributed to the long, successful run of *How Did This Get Made?* since its first episode in 2010.

This episode (which is no longer available to stream, as St. Clair forgot to plug her microphone into her computer, and her audio was lost), in addition to discussing a Christmas-themed romantic comedy, features the cast repeatedly wishing Mantzoukas a happy birthday. Throughout the episode, they surprise him with recorded video birthday greetings from friends as well as other entertainers he had endorsed on the podcast. These include Nick Kroll, a repeat podcast guest and a close friend of Mantzoukas; Annabeth Gish, an actress he has repeatedly praised and professed to have had a crush on in various podcast episodes; and Marisa Dabice, the singer and guitarist of the band Mannequin Pussy, whose song "Drunk II" Mantzoukas proclaimed "the song of the summer" in a 2019 episode of the podcast.

However, one of the birthday greetings was likely to be a surprise to fans who presumed they had a solid handle on Mantzoukas's media diet after regularly listening to him discuss his likes and dislikes for ten years. This came from Jordan Jones, about whom Mantzoukas enthused to listeners after the message. Jones offered a variety of suggestions on how to pass time alone under quarantine during the ongoing COVID-19 pandemic—all of them related to outdoor activities or craftsmanship—as Mantzoukas agreed with everything he said. After the video, Mantzoukas thanked Jones for the well-wishes and his friends for arranging it. He then explained to the podcast audience that Jones had appeared on the History series *Alone*, where competitors must survive in the wilderness with nothing but the items they bring with them, and whoever lasts the longest wins a cash prize. Mantzoukas encouraged his fans to watch the show, offering tips about which seasons were best (season 6, set in the Arctic, was the one Jones competed on, while seasons 4 and 5 were skippable), and detailed some of Jones's triumphs on the series. Most notable among these was having successfully hunted a moose armed only with a bow and arrow.

Each season of *Alone* follows a group of ten survivalists who attempt to, in terms of the show's introduction to each episode, "be the last one standing" in a given terrain. As indicated by the title, the isolation of the contestants is a key element of the series. They are not given any information about other competitors; they do not know how many people are still in the game or how they are faring. While they are in the same general vicinity, they do not encounter one another, and there is no camera crew for them to interact with. Contestants are responsible for carrying their own camera equipment and filming their experiences. They do have regular "well checks," in which a medical team checks their weight and other vital signs to ensure it is safe for them to continue competing. These mostly take place off-screen but are sometimes featured if they result in a contestant being forced to withdraw due to their body mass index falling below 17—a weight so low it puts them at risk of permanent organ or eyesight damage. At any time, a contestant may "tap out" by radioing to the crew that they wish to leave the show. This often occurs due to hunger, injury, or illness, but some contestants opt to leave for reasons like boredom or homesickness. Whoever is remaining when the others have all left receives a prize of $500,000.

Season 6 of *Alone* included three women and one Black man in its cast, but the majority of participants, as on *Forged in Fire*, were white men, as they have been across all seasons. The episodes heavily emphasize the dangerous and unforgiving nature of the Arctic landscape. Each episode opens with an on-screen quote related to challenge and survival. For example, the first episode of season 6 opens with "'Our food lies ahead and death stalks us from behind.'—Ernest Shackleton"; the sixth with "'The most difficult thing is the decision to act. The rest is merely tenacity.'—Amelia Earhart"; and the finale with "'One day, in retrospect, the years of struggle will strike you as the most beautiful.'—Sigmund Freud." After the aspirational framing of the quote, the show's introductory segment repeatedly highlights the extreme challenges of the terrain. There is a tracking shot of an ice- and snow-covered lake, then another of a snow-covered mountain peak, before the introductory voice-over begins: "In *Alone*'s coldest location ever, ten participants fight to survive the Arctic. Battling subzero temperatures, vicious predators, and isolation—how long will they endure? The last one standing wins." This narration is intercut with quick shots taken from the season's most dramatic moments—shots of wolves, injuries, fires, and storms—along with audio of various contestants describing the dangers they face and the fear they feel.

The language here is highly combative—the natural world is described as aggressive and even malevolent. Contestants must fight, battle, and face vicious opposition from the Arctic's landscape and fauna. This framing draws on a long-established narrative of American frontiersmanship in which nature is viewed as a chaotic force to be tamed by the intelligence and tenacity of a representative of the "civilized" world. This representative is generally a white man, a mythologized explorer/adventurer delving into unknown spaces. In keeping with the presidentially themed episode of *Forged in Fire* discussed earlier in this chapter, this image may be best signified by the statute of Theodore Roosevelt, which, in June 2020, the city of New York resolved to remove from the entrance of the Museum of Natural History (removal finally began in January of 2022). It depicted Theodore Roosevelt astride a horse, chest proudly forward with a confident look on his face, as a Native American man and an African man trail behind him on foot. Columbia University professor Mabel O. Wilson was quoted in a *New York Times* article about its removal that the statue "was clearly a narrative of white supremacy of domination" (Pogrebin). In spite of the decision to remove the statue, its initial installation at the Museum of Natural History demonstrates the intertwined histories of white supremacy, masculinity, and the impulse to view mankind's relationship to the natural world through the lens of "domination."

In spite of the ideological frame the show provides, contestants on *Alone* show a wider variety of perspectives and often demonstrate ambivalence about their relationship to the terrain in which they are attempting to establish themselves.

FIGURE 2 The Theodore Roosevelt statue in front of the American Museum of Natural History. (Credit: Public domain image, accessed from https://commons.wikimedia.org /wiki/File:Equestrian_Statue_of_Theodore_Roosevelt.jpg.)

Indeed, the contestant who most fully professes adherence to the idea of the experience of the Arctic as one of masculine combat is the first eliminated. In the first episode of season 6, Tim Backus refers to some of the other contestants (all attend a preparatory "boot camp" together before filming begins) as "wood nymphs and forest sages" whose interaction with the outdoors is akin to live-action role-playing games. He is careful to say that he likes them and appreciates that "they feel things from the heart," but that this is not his way. He announces the intention to honor their beliefs by asking for permission from and thanking the tree he will cut down, but it immediately becomes clear that Backus is using this as an opportunity for mockery. Holding the camera to frame an extreme close-up of his mouth inches from the tree, he affects a flirtatious tone and asks, "Hey, baby, how are you doing? Mind if I cut your kids down?" before laughing and saying, "That's stupid." He then turns to the camera he is holding and says, "See? Talking to trees is dumb." The scene then cuts to what is presumably a day or two later, as Backus decides to look for food. As he searches, he engages in another discourse about his masculinity, saying that while "berries and tea stuff" are good enough for some people, he is someone who likes to eat meat—"Burn it on the fire, crisp it up, and chomp it down." At this point, less than three minutes after he was shown mocking the spiritual beliefs of other contestants, he falls and breaks his leg. This injury necessitates Backus radioing for help and tapping out of the competition, making him the first to quit.

However, the show does not present respect for the natural world as a means of avoiding such karmic retribution. The second contestant to tap is Donny Dust, whose interactions with the Arctic terrain are conducted very differently than Backus's. In the second episode of season 6, Dust successfully shoots a muskrat with his bow and arrow. As he skins the muskrat and prepares it for consumption, he tells it, "Thank you, little dude. I appreciate it. I'm starving." This is not spoken with reverence or mockery, but with genuine affection. Dust is excited to have caught the muskrat, but he does not tie the success to his masculinity or any form of oppositional engagement with nature. In spite of the difference in attitude from Backus, this incident quickly brings about Dust's exit from the show. Shortly after eating the cooked muskrat, Dust becomes violently ill. An explanatory chyron on screen states, "Parasitic worms in meat can cause dysentery, cramping, and severe constipation." As his suffering drags on through the night and into the next day, Dust becomes concerned that this illness will aggravate a preexisting heart condition, and he makes the decision to tap out. Before radioing for help, he sits in front of the camera, weeping into his hat and apologizing to his wife and children. He cries as he explains to the crew that has come to get him that he is leaving because he is afraid for his health. However, in the voice-over (recorded later) that plays over the scene of his subsequent exit, Dust's attitude is more in line with that of participants leaving *Forged in Fire*. He states, "In every situation there's going to be positives and negatives, and you're gonna learn from both of them." He goes on to say, "I'm realizing it's OK to let the barriers down and it's OK to be human and ask somebody for help." Dust is far from the only contestant on *Alone* to openly display emotions.

The contestant who is depicted as most explicitly rejecting the oppositional framing between human and nature put forth by *Alone* is Woniya Thibeault, an ancestral skills instructor who several times throughout the series mentions her desire to demonstrate the effectiveness of a more feminine and cooperative understanding of the natural world. In her profile on History's website, she is described as someone who "believes in the coexistence of humans and nature and she comes to *Alone* both to test her skills and to demonstrate what is possible when one approaches survival from a place of respect, connection, and interdependence." Thibeault ultimately comes in second, tapping out after seventy-three days due to lack of food and her low weight. Of the five participants who remained on the series past the fifty-day mark, only one left for reasons other than starvation (this was Nathan Donnelly, who tapped after his shelter burned down). By the end of season 6, *Alone* was no longer tracking who could survive but who would starve to a medically threatening weight most slowly. Prior to Thibeault's exit, both Nikki van Schyndel and Barry Karcher were pulled from competition due to low weight.

On the show, Thibeault's decision to withdraw is framed as a choice informed primarily by a feeling of satisfaction with what she has accomplished and by respect for her physical limits. As she debates whether or not to leave the competition, she sits by the campfire and addresses the camera, saying, "I know how freaking skinny I am. I know it's not sustainable. So I know I have a really profound choice. What do I want to give myself, and what do I want to honor most? . . . I'm freaking starving, and I have been asking so much of my body. And it has been doing everything I ask of it. My body has given its all." At this point Thibeault appears undecided, but the next time she is seen, she is greeting the helicopter she called to pick her up. She weeps and explains that she has mixed feelings, but "looking at my body, I can just see how much it's given, and I know that it has given all that I want to ask it to right now." She goes on to say, "Today's my birthday, and it felt like the most amazing gift I could give myself—to put myself somewhere where I have warmth and food and the ability to care for myself." Thibeault's departure is thus framed by the show as being motivated by the desires that led her to participate: sustainability, compassion, and care. All these values are traditionally coded as feminine, and while *Alone* depicts them respectfully, it also uses Thibeault's reflections to emphasize them as the cause of her loss. In an interview with a local news station after the series aired, however, Thibeault offers a somewhat different, complementary explanation, that did not make it on the show: "I had a medical check later that day and I was fairly certain I was going to be pulled because I was so underweight, but I wanted it to be my choice" (McIntyre). Thibeault's desire for self-determination seems to not fit the show's narrative of her. Thibeault is one of several women to finish an *Alone* season in second place—so far, no woman has won a season.

The winner of season 6, Jordan Jones, is portrayed as embodying the rugged independence, tenacity, and humility regarded as ideal masculine traits of past and present by History's reality programs. As noted by Jason Mantzoukas after the birthday greeting, during the season Jones successfully hunts a moose using a bow and arrow, and later (off-screen) kills a wolverine with a hatchet. But he also recognizes the limits of his successes. Though he is one of the few contestants who is never shown crying during his time on the show, Jones does express pessimism toward the end of the season. In his own reflection, given to his camera in the final episode of the season, Jones notes that his success with the moose was not as beneficial as he had hoped it would be, since he then lost "who knows how many pounds of fat" to wolverines that stole the meat. He also describes his difficulty in catching fish as being dealt a "tough hand." He laments, "I don't have the body fat, I can't protect my meat, I'm helpless right now. . . . At this point, barring a miracle, I'm just done."

However, in spite of his resignation to being unable to continue, Jones attempts to strategize a means to avoid leaving the show. At this point the viewer knows Thibeault has left and that Jones is the winner, but Jones's attempts to remain competitive are included to illustrate his tenacity in the face of challenges, which contrasts with the show's framing of Thibeault opting to depart to provide herself the birthday gift of food and shelter. The day of the medical check at which he is told he has won, Jones is shown successfully ice fishing. As he cooks his fish over his fire, he tells the camera, "I've been thinking all night about what I'm going to say to them to try to convince them that I'm fine." When asked by the team sent to evaluate him how he is feeling, Jones immediately launches into an attempt to rationalize his low weight, saying, "I'm one of the tallest, thinnest, but also strong people that I know. . . . So I'm actually really fit when I'm lean. I literally think I can be healthily lighter than anyone else out here." As he talks, he is approached from behind by his wife, there to surprise him with the news that he is the last contestant remaining. In this moment, the show makes Jones's desire to continue competing, even under adverse conditions that he has labeled as hopeless, the defining element of his victory.

Although *Alone* is unscripted, each participant generates hundreds or even thousands of hours of footage (with the amount depending on how many days they remain in competition). The program's narrative arc is shaped through editing choices. The choice of which moments of reflection, good fortune, or bad luck to feature, as well as which participants' other successes, failures, or attempts to allay boredom to set them against, is entirely the prerogative of the editors. As demonstrated through its depiction of Backus's exaggerated portrayal of masculinity and rapid exit from the program, *Alone* does reject the same forms of toxic masculinity that *Forged in Fire* excludes from its series. However, it maintains an ethos of white male superiority, focusing instead on tenacity, self-taught skills, and emotional control. All the contestants who exit the program are clearly shown to have fallen short of one of these values prior to their exit, and only the season's ultimate winner is depicted as consistent and unflinching in the face of nature's indifferent brutality. Jones is depicted as embodying what is imagined as a "frontier spirit" in the historical imaginary; the same form of masculinity believed to have driven westward expansion allows Jones to be unique and successful in the present.

Conclusion

The History channel's most popular reality programs, *Forged in Fire* and *Alone*, provide a means of examining how the historical imaginary, mass media, and history constellate around understandings of hegemonic masculine identity. Jackson Katz describes the widely perceived contemporary "crisis in masculinity" as "what happens to some men—and groups of men—when technological, geopolitical, religious, and other systemic and historical changes disrupt old gender hierarchies and social structures, establishing new gender norms and forging new identities." *Forged in Fire* and *Alone* have achieved and maintained popularity in part by eschewing some of the typical markers of hypermasculinity, particularly outward competitiveness and macho self-aggrandizement. However, they have also worked to reify and resolidify white masculine identity through a depiction of skills, tenacity, and material knowledge as the unchanging and defining traits of white men, past and present.

2

Time Travel
Television Series

• •

One of the most recent frameworks for exploring cultural relations to temporality is the concept of time travel, which has maintained a presence in science fiction, with moments of intensified mass popularity, since its introduction in the late nineteenth century. There were isolated instances of stories of individuals being somehow temporally displaced, generally by sleeping for an extremely long time (most famously Washington Irving's Rip Van Winkle), prior to the publication of Edward Page Mitchell's short story "The Clock That Went Backward" and H. G. Wells's novel *The Time Machine* (which is credited with simultaneously popularizing both the device of time travel and the new genre of science fiction). However, the idea of being voluntarily transported through time by mechanical means, with the possibility of returning to one's temporal point of origin, is an invention of the industrial age. As James Gleick writes in *Time Travel: A History*, "Time travel feels like an ancient tradition, rooted in old mythologies, old as gods and dragons. It isn't. . . . When Wells, in his lamp-lit room imagined a time machine, he also invented a new mode of thought. Why not before? And why now?" (4–5). I will begin my examination of time travel narratives and the historical imaginary with this question and will go on to consider how different permutations of Wells's new mode of thought have been taken up in recent years. This chapter examines a recent surge in the popularity of time travel, particularly in television series, that reached its peak in 2016. By analyzing several series that use the device of time travel to allow a representative of the present to directly engage the past (*11.22.63*,

Timeless, Making History, and *Legends of Tomorrow*), I explore how popular narratives of time travel intervene in the historical imaginary, both in its depictions of the past and, more important, in the direct connections they draw between the past and the present moment. Unlike previously dominant narratives of time travel, which tended to focus on interventions by everyday people into the past in order to avert an unhappy future, these time travel series foreground historians and educators venturing into the past in order to preserve it, and thus maintain the status quo of the present. These representations of the existing past as both necessary and in need of protection from historians serve the function of the historical imaginary to shore up national identity by smoothing over the traumatic histories that, as Walter Benjamin wrote, are "flashing up" at us in depicting them as unpleasant but necessary in the formation of the best possible present moment.

It seems clear that at least part of the answer to Gleick's question of why time travel fiction emerged in the late nineteenth century is rooted in the proliferation of technologies that allowed the easy capture and unlimited reproduction of moments in time: the camera and early cinema. René Thoreau Bruckner writes that "time travel is a fantasy that seems to stem directly, and quite simply, from our habit of spatializing time" (2), and it was through camera technologies that moments of time became understandable as objects that could be held, manipulated, examined, and relived. As Walter Benjamin argues in "The Work of Art in the Age of Its Technological Reproducibility," these technologies taught new ways of perceiving the world and daily life through "all its resources for swooping and rising, disrupting and isolating, stretching or compressing a sequence, enlarging or reducing an object. . . . It is through the camera that we first discover the optical unconscious" (37). The sense of mastery over time that is available through the camera—that it may be frozen, sped up, slowed down, and indefinitely replayed—almost certainly lies at the root of the idea that one may, through mechanical means, overcome the bounds of temporality to journey backward or forward in time.

Bruckner understands the drive to time travel in terms of Freud's "A Note upon the Mystic Writing Pad." Published in 1925 (only a few decades after time travel emerged as a popular device in fiction), Freud's essay argues that time and consciousness are ineluctably bound with one another; both our consciousness and our understanding of time emerge in the organizing of perceptions into memories. Neuroses arise from repressed memories, which are "timeless," and it is only by revisiting these memories on the analyst's couch/time machine that an individual has "hope of destroying the timelessness of which neuroses are made and putting 'time' there instead: mutability, the possibility of progress, transformation" (Bruckner 8). Building on Freud's description of the relation between desire and time consciousness, Bruckner argues that time as spatialized in time travel fiction may be best understood as having a spiral shape: "One never passes directly through an already-past moment a second time but is always reeling toward one and always reeling away at the same time. . . . The spiral envisions the relationship between present and past as one of proximity, of swinging past, a perpetual tease" (11). As such, history never exactly repeats—one may pass by the same moment again, but the traveler has been altered by their experiences and is thus shifted to a parallel but removed space on the spiral. There is no true return to the previous point, and attempting to reach it only offers longing and frustration. These themes emerge repeatedly across all the series I examine here—time travelers who intensely desire to occupy the past (because of either their interest in the era or their emotional attachment to someone in it) are left in some way unhappy and unfulfilled by their experiences outside of their own temporality.

This idea of time travel as providing "a perpetual tease" emerges again and again in narratives that feature the device. Given its origin, it is unsurprising that while time travel has remained a reasonably popular device in literature, its best-known uses have been on-screen. Several television series of the 1960s—*The Twilight Zone* (1959–1964), *Star Trek* (1966–1969), and *Doctor Who* (1963–1989)—remain among the most iconic examples of time travel. The most memorable instances of time travel's perpetual tease include *The Twilight Zone*'s episode "Walking Distance," in which a man returns to an idealized summer of his youth only to be told by his father he must return to the present, and *Star Trek*'s episode "The City on the Edge of Forever," in which, after traveling through time to the 1930s, Captain Kirk must allow a woman he loves to die to prevent Germany from winning World War II. Many of the most famous films to feature time travel were made in the 1980s, which saw the release of the *Back to the Future* films and the beginning of the *Terminator* saga, as well as *Time Bandits* (1981); *Star Trek IV* (1986), which is centered on using time travel to save humpback whales; *Bill and Ted's Excellent Adventure* (1989); and numerous others. The most iconic of these films centered on a time traveler returning to the past to prevent an unwelcome future. In *The Terminator* (1984) and its first sequel *Terminator 2: Judgment Day* (1991), time travelers come from the future to affect the outcome of a robot uprising that will soon take place, while *Back to the Future*'s (1985) Marty McFly ultimately turns his parents from unhappy schlubs to fashionable successes. These films engage specific anxieties of the Reagan era—the apocalyptic future of *The Terminator* resonates strongly with Cold War anxieties of nuclear annihilation, and the use of the McFlys' transformation to signify the happy ending of *Back to the Future* illustrates fears of being left behind in a time of increasingly conspicuous material consumption.

Andrew Gordon argues that the proliferation of time travel films in the 1980s was indicative of a broader cultural belief that society had taken a wrong turn, and that the past was a more desirable space to inhabit: "These time-travel films rarely attempt a vision of the future, and when they do, as in *The*

Terminator, the future is bleak and post-apocalyptic. . . . They reflect a growing dissatisfaction with a present that is sensed as dehumanized, diseased, out of control, and perhaps doomed. Somewhere along the line, the unspoken feeling goes, something went drastically wrong; if we could only return to the appropriate crossroads in the past and correct things, we could mend history and return to a revised, glorious present or future, the time line we truly deserve" (373). This idea, that the present can be corrected through an intervention in the past, seemingly runs counter to what David Wittenberg identifies as "the 'conservative' characteristic of time travel fiction," which, he argues, "tends to restore histories rather than to destroy or subvert them" (2). However, the root of the distinction lies in the scale of the history being changed; time travel fiction generally allows the characters to improve their personal circumstances— as Marty McFly does in *Back to the Future* by improving his parents' love story, or as the protagonist in *About Time* (2013) does by using his ability to return to his own past to improve his romantic fortunes. But time travel fictions that engage directly with historical events—rather than with daily life in the past or future—almost universally portray the past as something that must be preserved, as in *Star Trek*'s "The City on the Edge of Forever," or that apparently is immune to intervention, as in *Doctor Who*. Jerome de Groot describes *Doctor Who* and other depictions of time travel that do not "consider movement *between* times so much as movement *to* particular periods" as treating the past as "simply a backdrop to have the particular episodes' narrative projected onto rather than inextricably intertwined with the events unfolding" (*Remaking History* 240). He argues that the most interesting time travel series are those that consider the relation between past and present, rather than simply treating other times as destinations.

The recent surge in time travel fiction, unlike the 1980s film wave examined by Gordon, has primarily been in television series that in some way examine the relationship between past and present. Television has long been a popular site for examining the past; as Malgorzata Rymsza-Pawlowska points out, "Because of the medium's unique relationship with history and temporality, developments in television programming are a particularly apt site at which to examine shifts in American understandings of and relationships with the past" (83). Rymsza-Pawlowska writes that because of the television format's shared characteristics with time—particularly its ongoing nature, as described in Raymond Williams's idea of television's "flow"—it serves as a particularly apt site for understanding the continual progression of time. Williams describes flow as "the defining characteristic of broadcasting, simultaneously as a technology and as a cultural form," (86). Flow is the means by which television programs and their embedded advertisements serve capitalist interest by encouraging viewers to remain engaged with a viewing experience that can continue indefinitely.

If we accept this reasoning as part of the popularity of the straightforward depictions of the past on television (i.e., without time travel) described by Rymsza-Pawlowska, then it seems likely that the form of television's current moment—which is increasingly defined by on-demand streaming services and binge-watching—plays a role in the sudden popularity of time travel narratives. Williams described flow during the network era of television, which required the maintenance of a continuity of experience for the viewer between programs, ads, and the programs that followed. This viewing formation has since been largely interrupted by streaming services, which tend not to include ads or programs that feed in to one another, or devices like TiVo, which allow viewers to pause, fast-forward, and rewind shows as they watch. Like the time traveler, contemporary viewers find themselves suddenly empowered to escape the long-prevailing logics of flow; as the time traveler is free to traverse the timeline, the viewer is free to jump between episodes, revisit favorites, and skip what is not engaging. This parallel may be useful in understanding the current surge of time travel television series. Two of the three series that pioneered the genre of time travel television, *Doctor Who* and *Star Trek*, have recently returned to the air, and just since 2015 numerous other series centered around time travel have been released, including *Timeless* (2016–2018), *Travelers* (2016–2018), *11.22.63* (2016), *Legends of Tomorrow* (2016–present), *Dark* (2017–2020), *12 Monkeys* (2015–2018), *Making History* (2017), and *Time after Time* (2017). Not all of these series have been successful—*Time after Time*, which centered on H. G. Wells following Jack the Ripper from the nineteenth century to 2017, aired only five episodes. However, if nothing else, the sheer quantity of serialized time travel programs suddenly available seems indicative of an increased interest in the ways in which histories reverberate through each other and lines of continuity between the past and present, raising the question of how things may have been different today if past individuals had made different choices.

Unlike the nineteenth-century science fiction in which the idea of a time travel device first emerged, which is broadly defined by a sense of optimism concerning human innovation and exploration, science fiction on-screen is often perceived as a largely pessimistic genre. Vivian Sobchack critiques this position as an oversimplification but also points out that science fiction films "only emerged as a critically recognized genre *after* Hiroshima" and that "the film genre, emerging when it did, had no roots in the philosophical attitudes of the nineteenth century" (*Screening Space* 21). The uses and meaning of time travel, or any depiction of temporality, are highly specific to their own times. This idea is well established in examinations of screened history; Robert Burgoyne writes that any depiction of history, "like the mythic image of Janus, looks to both the past and the present" (11). But this is especially true of time travel narratives, which relate directly to the present moment; almost all protagonists of such narratives are contemporary with their intended audience, and as such their adventure is directly filtered through the present in a way other period films do not have to be.

In this chapter I examine the Hulu miniseries *11.22.63* and the NBC series *Timeless*, as well as two programs that use time travel's interventions in history to comedic effect, *Making History* and *Legends of Tomorrow*. Each of these shows focuses on a protagonist or a team of protagonists from our own time who use time travel to directly intervene in the past. Unlike Marty McFly of *Back to the Future*, these series' travelers are seeking some form of direct engagement with well-known historical events and figures; their time travel missions are fueled not by their domestic lives but by an interest in significant moments in national history. While some of these programs contain moments of subversive potential in their depictions of how the past unfolds and how we come to understand history, each ultimately adheres to the conservative impulse identified by Wittenberg and portrays the preservation of known history as an ultimate good. As such, unlike previous depictions of time travel that idealized the past as a space of possibility (i.e., where positive changes could and should occur), these series present an exalted view of the present moment as the past's best possible outcome—individuals who have devoted themselves to the study of history find their desire to explore the past or change the present can only be harmful. These series' interventions into the historical imaginary discourage anything more than a cursory glance toward the past, alleviating discomfort by depicting it as flawed but familiar, and arguing that the history we know is simply what was meant to be.

11.22.63

The miniseries *11.22.63*, based on a Stephen King novel of the same name, is centered on Jake Epping (James Franco), a high school teacher who is persuaded to travel to 1960 to preemptively investigate and avert the assassination of President John Kennedy. Rather than a time machine, Jake travels through an unexplained portal in the closet of a diner owned by his friend Al. Anyone leaving through the portal always arrives at 11:58 A.M. on October 21, 1960, and, regardless of how long they stay, returns two minutes from the time of their departure. Traveling to 1960 resets the timeline; any changes that may have been effected on previous journeys are erased. Al, a Vietnam veteran, believes that Kennedy's survival will prevent the escalation in Vietnam overseen by President Lyndon Johnson, saving numerous lives and leading to a better world. He has been attempting to use the portal to accomplish this himself but succumbs to terminal cancer before he is able to do so. Armed with Al's notes about the assassination and tips on how to blend in once he arrives in the past, Jake travels to 1960 to investigate Lee Harvey Oswald and prevent the assassination. Along the way, he falls in love with a Texas librarian named Sadie.

The series' opening credit sequence features a scale model of the site of the Kennedy assassination, with a long strand of red string weaving together various key objects—the car, the gun, the clock—and connecting various newspaper articles and cut-out images of the key players. These items, the fragile pieces of some (possibly only perceived) conspiracy, tacked to walls and connected with a web of red threads, make up an image so strongly associated with paranoia and delusion it has been endlessly subject to pastiche. However, much of *11.22.63* is premised on Jake, and by extension the viewer, taking the question of who is responsible for Kennedy's death seriously rather than (as Jake initially does) scoffing at the decades of obsession and theories as the purview of cranks. Nothing in the opening credits immediately connotes the idea of time travel. All details point instead to a conspiracy theorist obsessed with a famous event, someone who might constantly long for the ability to revisit the moment and find out what really happened but will never be able to fully re-create it. The vast majority of the series is much more focused on the intrigues of the Kennedy assassination and the events leading up to it than on the time travel that enables Jake to reluctantly fulfill the dream of the model's creator. In its telling of those events, the series draws on the understandings of this period as it has been repeatedly portrayed and solidified in the historical imaginary rather than disrupting them—the intrigues of the FBI and CIA; the bright, messianic figure of Kennedy; the troubled, increasingly threatening Oswald; and the general air of Russian-accented Cold War machinations.

Because the portal Jake travels through will only place him on October 21, 1960, he must spend three years waiting for the date of the assassination in order to avert it. Events often do not go as he wishes, but he cannot return to the present day and reset the timeline without losing all progress he may have made, along with the relationships he has formed (in addition to his romance with Sadie, Jake is befriended and helped by Bill, another "native" of the 1960s). As such, of *11.22.63*'s eight episodes, only the first and last directly depict time travel. In the intervening episodes, Jake benefits less and less from the advantages of having traveled in time—he loses Al's notes early on in his adventure, and his knowledge of upcoming events is less useful as he is increasingly enmeshed in daily life of the early 1960s. Indeed, his adjustment to the past is remarkably smooth; the show quickly moves beyond Jake's surprise at the low prices and momentary frown at a segregated restroom he encounters in his journey from Maine to Texas.

Once settled in Dallas, Jake rarely takes note of the differences between the time he now inhabits and the world as he has known it, and when he does, his response is usually mild irritation. One exception occurs in the third episode, "Other Voices, Other Rooms," when Jake encounters Miss Mimi, a Black

FIGURE 3 Jake Epping storms toward his car after berating a racist gas station attendant as Miss Mimi looks on. (Credit: Screenshot from *11.22.63*.)

woman and a member of the administrative staff in the high school where he is teaching; she has run out of gas and walked twelve blocks to the station Jake happens to be near to buy some. Prior to this moment, the episode includes a scene where the entire school office comes to a silent and scandalized halt when Jake offers to get Miss Mimi a cup of coffee, which she politely declines (thus defusing the situation). In that moment, Jake's only response was to roll his eyes and grit his teeth at the petty racism of the time he is in. However, after the gas station attendant refuses to sell gas to Miss Mimi or to Jake acting on her behalf, he snaps. Jake shoves the attendant, seizes his arm, and yells, "Why don't you shut your f-cking mouth?" before helping himself to the gas can and throwing the money for it on the ground. The station attendant is cowed and bewildered, and though Jake smiles politely at Miss Mimi as he opens the door to his car for her to drive her back to her own vehicle, she appears concerned.

Miss Mimi appears as a minor character in four episodes of *11.22.63*, and it is solely through her that the show addresses questions of race. Through her characterization, and Jake's friendship with her, the show reflects one of the primary narratives white hegemonic ideology tells about itself to rationalize racial inequality: that white people are actually more invested in racial equality than Black people are. This belief is one of the narratives described by Eithne Quinn in "Sincere Fictions: The Production Cultures of Whiteness in Late 1960s Hollywood" as "open[ing] up new ways of explaining continuing inequalities that were much harder to pin down than the Jim Crow practices of old defended by law" (5). In moments like the ones just described, *11.22.63* is critical of Jim Crow segregation, but its critique is filtered through a portrayal of white nobility that took root, as noted by Quinn, the moment Jim Crow ended.

As the show's representative of Black Americans living during segregation, Miss Mimi is portrayed as perceptive, kind, and—above all—dignified. In the fourth episode, "The Eyes of Texas," she tells Jake that misleading people denies them their dignity, and in a moment the show gives significant weight (through the background music, the emotional quaver in Miss Mimi's voice, and the lingering close-up on her face as she delivers the line), she tells him, "And for some of us, dignity matters." However, one aspect of the portrayal of Miss Mimi as dignified is her unwavering acceptance of the social circumstances she finds herself in. Miss Mimi consistently finds Jake's moments of disruption to established racial hierarchies on her behalf unsettling, though the show gives no indication of potential consequences to either character arising from them. She is also portrayed as the only Black person existing in an entirely white space— she is employed at a segregated school for white students, maintains a cautiously friendly but professional relationship with Jake, and is engaged in a secret long-term affair with the school's white principal (Mr. Simmons). When she confides to Jake that she has terminal cancer and Mr. Simmons wants to take her to Mexico to pursue experimental treatment, she dismisses the idea with a smirk saying, "That's just borrowing trouble." Her final requests to Jake are to be a friend to Mr. Simmons after her death, and to not hesitate to pursue happiness in his relationship with Sadie. Miss Mimi's choice to adhere to the hegemonic social order that oppresses her, in spite of the multiple white men in her life urging her to step outside of it (in both significant and minor ways), could be an opportunity for the show to note the uneven risks of such resistance: Jake and Mr. Simmons face significantly less danger than Miss Mimi for such choices. However, *11.22.63* never alludes to any potential pushback to these moments, and thus Miss Mimi serves as a tragic figure purely to motivate and develop the emotional interiority of the white male characters she interacts with. In its attempt to portray Miss Mimi as sympathetic and dignified, *11.22.63* ultimately depicts its only significant Black character as resistant to the racially progressive interventions of the white men who want to help.

Jake shares a frame of reference with the viewer, but the knowledge he brings from the future often fails to help him. In contrast to typical depictions of time travel, where information or technology from the future provides a significant advantage for the time traveler (such as Biff in *Back to the Future Part II* (1989), who builds a fortune winning bets on sporting events for which he knows the outcome, or Ash in *Army of Darkness* (1992), who cows the medieval peasantry with his shotgun/"boom stick"), Jake frequently scrambles to simply pass as an everyday individual. While his primary interest is in averting the Kennedy assassination, the nature of the rabbit hole forces him to embed himself in the past while he waits for that event, and his broader historical knowledge in no way prepares him to cope with the emotional attachments he forms in the community he becomes a part of. His lies are exposed numerous times: first by

Bill, then by Miss Mimi when she attempts to verify his credentials for employment at the high school, by Sadie when she discovers surveillance equipment in his house, and by Mr. Simmons when Jake is arrested. In most instances, he offers some weak excuse, but ultimately it is the other characters' fondness for him that causes them to forgive his deception, rather than any superior knowledge or insight he brings. When he and Sadie are attacked by her abusive ex-husband, for example, there is no advantage to Jake in having come from the future. This serves to underscore the view of history the show presents through Jake's lecture to an inattentive high school class in the series' first episode: "People tend to think the important stories are wars, elections, political movements—but these [unknown] people matter. The little things matter."

However, Jake, along with the audience, is never permitted to forget his status as a man out of place in time. While most of the show's plot revolves around Jake and Bill's investigation of Oswald, the soon-to-be assassin is not the villain of the series. Instead, that role is filled by time, which continually resists Jake's interventions in history and attempts to maintain the past as we know it. Al explains this to Jake as time "pushing back." Throughout the series, seemingly random and often violent events interfere with Jake, Bill, and Sadie. Going into a restaurant in the first episode, Jake must avoid being set on fire by a knocked-over candle igniting a drink near his suit, and a heavy chandelier nearly falls on him (in addition to the smaller inconveniences of having to bribe the maître d'; the interruptions of a persistently overly friendly waitress; and the interfering noise of a blender, laughter, and a dropped tray of glasses as he tries to eavesdrop). A random fire consumes the house he is staying in, destroying Al's notes and killing the landlady's young son. Cars drive off the road, nearly mowing Jake down, and strangers frequently tell him, "You shouldn't be here." At various important moments, Jake, Bill, and Sadie are all distracted by visions of people from their past who have died, which "time" conjures to thwart them, and Sadie is nearly killed during surgery after her ex-husband's violent assault necessitates her hospitalization. The presence of "time," or its active/vengeful intervention in a given moment, is typically signified by a general sense of foreboding, a look of panic from Jake, or the nondiegetic sound of high-pitched music. However, the show makes this interference by "time" explicit rather than ambiguous—we are given no reason to doubt that Al and Jake are correct in that the timeline is attempting to right itself, and in the finale this is confirmed by the "yellow card man" Jake frequently glimpses at the moment of time's intercedence in events.

These dangers work throughout the series to disrupt the perception of the past as an idealized space that viewers, whose familiarity with time travel is likely based on the movies of the 1980s wave, may be primed to expect. Initially, in the first episode ("Rabbit Hole"), *11.22.63* depicts the present as dull and disaffecting, and Jake's life as one he should be eager to escape. Before Jake visits

1960, every scene is dominated by the color gray, and the characters are universally unhappy—some bored, some cruel, and some unfairly disadvantaged. Jake's students nap and watch cell phone videos as he tries to teach, he is recently divorced, and his father died while he was on the plane going to tell him goodbye. The city he lives in appears dilapidated, with boarded-up windows and empty streets. When Jake passes through, as Al terms it, "the rabbit hole," to arrive in 1960, he is suddenly awash in sunshine and surrounded by bustling industry. A factory whistle blows, and blue-collar workers cheerfully mill about. Jake's eye is immediately drawn to various signifiers of wholesomeness and Americana, particularly a milkman in a pristine white uniform, and a trio of beautiful, giggling blonde women driving by in a pink convertible. The montage of Jake initially exploring 1960 is set to the Paul Evans song "Happy-Go-Lucky Me," as Jake delights in delicious food and the low prices of the apparent paradise he now inhabits. But this view of the past is short-lived. As evening falls and Jake arrives in a bar on the wrong side of town, the laughter in "Happy-Go-Lucky Me" takes on ominous tones as the city darkens. The saturated colors of Jake's initial arrival in the past do not return, and while they are not as gray as scenes from the present, the remainder of the scenes from 1960 to 1963 are mainly shot in more subdued tones, particularly blues and greens.

In the final episode ("The Day in Question"), Jake successfully saves President Kennedy, but Sadie is accidentally killed as he confronts Oswald. Jake resolves to reset the timeline and try again, assuming that he will now be able to save both Kennedy and Sadie. To do so, Jake must first return to 2016, where he sees the results of Kennedy's survival. However, the present, unlike the improved world Al envisioned, is now a postapocalyptic wasteland. This version of 2016 is far bleaker than the grim present of "The Rabbit Hole," which, by comparison to the world Jake has created, no longer seems gray or run-down. The diner is gone, most buildings are flattened, and groups of violent scavengers wander around, assaulting whoever they encounter. Their faces are obscured, both by filth and by the gray haze that permeates the air. Jake discovers that after Kennedy served two terms, George Wallace was elected president, and before the end of the 1970s, life as it was known was shattered by global bombings and widespread, horrific suffering. Jake returns to the rabbit hole and transports himself back to the reset point in 1960, thus returning the timeline to its original, unaltered version. He returns to the light- and color-saturated version of an apparently perfect past, where he now recognizes one of the three blonde women in the convertible as Sadie and races after her, intent on finding a way to live their love story again.

However, Jake is dissuaded from any attempt to reshape the past again by "the yellow card man," another time traveler who warns him that while he may tell himself things will be different, "It's always the same loop. It goes and it goes. . . . It's always the same end." Jake swears, increasingly desperate, that he will not save Kennedy or interfere with history; he simply wants to be with Sadie. However, the other traveler insists that Jake's involvement with Sadie will always lead to her death, and so Jake returns, heartbroken, to 2016, leaving the past unaltered. He eventually looks up Sadie and discovers that she is receiving an award for her lifetime of service to her community, and he travels from Maine to Texas to see her accept it. In her acceptance speech, she reads a poem that summarizes the series' theme of relating to our own temporality:

> We did not ask for this room or this music. We were invited in.
> Therefore, because the dark surrounds us, let us turn our faces to the light.
> Let us endure hardship, to be grateful for plenty.
> We have been given pain, to be astounded by joy.
> We have been given life, to deny death.
> We did not ask for this room, or this music.
> But because we are here, let us dance.

The poem is original to the series, though presented as if it were a well-known standard. The clear implication here is that life is a gift to be enjoyed, and to dwell on the imperfections of a moment is folly. This is not an especially controversial philosophical position, but in relation to the series' treatment of history and time, it further emphasizes the idea that individuals should concern themselves with interpersonal relationships rather than the broader circumstances of their moment. Those who insist on how things could be better, like Al and the unnamed time traveler who urges Jake to escape the loop he is embarking on while remaining in his own, are destroyed by their fixation on changing "this room, or this music" to what they would have "asked" for.

At one point during her recitation, Sadie is shown from behind, silhouetted by a spotlight shining on her. This is an echo of how John F. Kennedy is depicted in "The Rabbit Hole," when Jake attends one of his speeches. While the various shots of Kennedy seem designed primarily to obscure the actor portraying him, the re-creation of that moment here emphasizes Sadie as an equally important figure. Ultimately, the show offers a view of the past as immutable, and the act of looking (or traveling) back as inherently counterproductive. Tragically, Jake is forced to bid farewell to his vision of a life with Sadie, but because she has lived only in her own moment, she has been able to be happy.

Timeless

The NBC series *Timeless*, like *11.22.63*, premiered in 2016 and is centered on an educator who travels to the past. The circumstances presented, however, are very different; in *Timeless*, Lucy, a professor of history, is recruited by government agents to aid in the capture of Flynn, a terrorist who has stolen one of the two time machines in existence. Along with Wyatt, a soldier, and Rufus, one of the engineers who designed the time machines, Lucy must use the remaining time machine to follow Flynn to different points in history and try to prevent him from altering the timeline. While the show's plot grows increasingly complicated over the course of its two seasons, the consistent conflict is between villains who wish to change the past to suit their goals, and heroes who work to maintain the current timeline, even when that requires significant sacrifice. In each episode, the team travels to a different location in time—as recently as the 1980s and as far back as the Salem witch trials of the late seventeenth century—and simultaneously works to thwart Flynn (and later a broader shadow-government conspiracy) while leaving the past unaltered. Within the mythology of the show, it is fatal for an individual to pass through their own timeline—thus, characters cannot travel back to moments in which they have lived or previously traveled. In their first mission, Flynn causes the airship Hindenburg to complete its initial journey without incident, and upon returning to the present, Lucy finds that as a result of that alteration to the timeline, her sister no longer exists. Lucy continues her missions, determined to restore her sister and stop Flynn. Whenever the past is altered, only those who have journeyed through time retain memories of how it is "supposed" to be; when they return, the new history is the only one those who remained in the present are aware of. The losses triggered by these changes tend to be exclusively personal; other effects of the team's adventures often are humorous or without meaningful impact. For example, after the episode "Party at Castle Varlar," in which the team encounters a young Ian Fleming, they return to the present to find there is now a James Bond novel based on their exploits with the author/spy.

Lucy's role on the team as a historian is twofold—because of her knowledge of past events, she knows how history is "supposed" to unfold and can thus prevent the crew from inadvertently altering major events. In the world of *Timeless*, historians carry within them an encyclopedic knowledge of every detail of every past event and era, and the show makes much of Lucy's obsessive devotion to the minutiae of the past. She is also tasked with using her expertise to make sure that she and her team blend in to each era; she explains customs and social expectations, though the team rarely faces much difficulty in acclimating to other periods. This is in spite of the fact that Rufus is Black and frequently expresses displeasure and irritation at the increased dangers he faces in traveling to times of segregation or slavery.

Rufus's unhappiness is generally treated as a source of humor. During their time in 1937 in the series' pilot episode, Rufus quips, "Well, the back of the bus was great," as Lucy gleefully marvels at exploring the past and grimaces when she apologetically advises him, "Don't make eye contact with anyone" while he waits outside the bar she and Wyatt are entering. Rufus's catharsis for these indignities comes later in the episode, when he says the

FIGURE 4 Rufus berates a racist police officer from a 1937 jail cell. (Credit: Screenshot from *Timeless*.)

following to a racist cop who repeatedly calls him "boy": "I'm in the damn stone age. But man, I hope you live a long, long life. Long enough to see Michael Jordan dunk, Michael Jackson dance, Mike Tyson punch—really just any Black guy named Michael. O.J.? Yeah, he gets off! He did it, but we don't care. And Obama? He's the president! 2008. That's gonna suck for you! I hope you see it all. Because the future is not on your side, boy." In this moment, the future is presented as compensation for the history of discrimination and violence. It is positioned as an empowering moment for Rufus as Lucy and Wyatt look on from another jail cell, Wyatt smiling, Lucy with her mouth agape in shock. The cop is clearly bewildered, but unhappy that Rufus is somehow getting the better of him.

This list of accomplishments is, in some ways, a very strange one for challenging the racism of the late 1930s. There is little doubt that if this police officer were to live long enough to see O. J. Simpson's acquittal, he would be unhappy about it, but this monologue seems to position that verdict as a civil rights victory on a par with Barack Obama's election rather than part of the kind of persistent, systemic racism that this officer would be right at home in. Similarly, while there would certainly be aspects of Michael Jackson's celebrity that would meet with this cop's disapproval, the existence of successful Black entertainers would not be shocking, as they existed then too. That Rufus does not draw on school integration, the Voting Rights Act, or the legalization of interracial marriage is indicative of how *Timeless* reinforces the historical imaginary's toned-down vision of the history of racism—that it was an issue of interpersonal unpleasantness rather than extreme, systemic oppression. This one racist is counterbalanced by the future successes of individual Black men.

Rufus's anger about traveling through the past while leaving the tragedies experienced by Black Americans unaltered is explored in the episode "The Assassination of Abraham Lincoln." Rufus insists to Lucy that they should just "shoot this asshat [Booth], save Lincoln here and now." When she argues that "it might change things too much," he asserts that "there might be a lot less lynchings" and that she is protecting "rich, white guys' history." He points out that as a Black man, "a lot of my history sucks." Lucy makes an impassioned plea for maintaining known history, warning against possible consequences of altering the past as incurred in *11.22.63*: "We would come back to an entirely different world. Who knows if it would be better, or if there would be anything left to come back to at all? The present isn't perfect, but it's ours. Awful as it is, what happens to Lincoln is meant to be." However, at the moment of the assassination, Lucy does try to save Lincoln. She is unable to do so, and events remain largely unchanged. This episode introduces a discussion of fate to the series, which, while not nearly as omnipresent as the interference of "time" in *11.22.63*, does play a role in understanding what should and should not be allowed to happen. When Lucy returns to the time machine, shaken, guilt-ridden, and with Lincoln's blood still staining her dress, Rufus comforts her, confirming that there was nothing she could do. He confirms that Lincoln's death and the violent oppression of Black Americans that followed are unavoidable tragedies of history. Similar to in his interaction with a racist police officer in the 1930s, Rufus again offers the present/future as compensation for the wrongs of the past; he attempts to comfort a Black soldier with the promise that eventually, things will get better. That the improvements he is referring to will not occur within that soldier's lifetime is left unspoken by the show.

Almost all episodes of *Timeless* include members of the team encountering major historical figures, including individuals as varied as Abraham Lincoln, the actress Hedy Lamarr, and John Hinkley Jr. Rather than the idea of ordinary people living their daily lives as the true stuff of history, as in *11.22.63*, *Timeless* zealously commits to a "great men and women" view of the past, and history as the events that arise from the actions of special individuals. This is established from Lucy's introduction early on in the pilot. She is seen lecturing a class and telling the students that when asked why America was in Vietnam, President Johnson responded by stating that his penis ("It's true, he called it jumbo") was the reason. She explains that these stories are "real history," and "to understand it, we've gotta get inside these people's heads. Their loves, their quirks, their 'jumbos.'" Her expertise in history throughout the series is repeatedly demonstrated in her knowledge of the details of world-historical people's lives. In "The Assassination of Abraham Lincoln," Wyatt challenges her certainty of what will happen that day, asking, "So Booth walks into Ford's

Theatre at exactly ten A.M.? Not nine fifty-six? Not ten oh-seven?" She immediately brushes aside the possibility, telling him, "Hundreds of books have been written about Booth's movements today" and they all agree that he arrived at the theater at precisely ten.

The idea that historians could know the exact moment that Booth checked his mail on the morning of the assassination is outlandish for any number of reasons. Prominent among them is the fact that standard time was a new development in the nineteenth century (Lincoln was assassinated in 1865, and U.S. time zones were not established until 1883); many towns still used the sun to set their local time, and variations were common. The times 9:56, 10:00, and 10:07 were likely to fall within an acceptable margin of error for people living their day-to-day lives (Andrewes). But this instance illustrates the ways in which *Timeless* portrays the past as anachronistically legible in terms of the present and significantly misrepresents the work of historians, who within the series serve solely as a repository of dates, times, and trivia.

Like *11.22.63*, *Timeless* presents the past as a space that should not be interfered with, as that interference poses a threat to the present moment. Any alteration is seen, particularly by Lucy, as detrimental. Lucy's protectiveness of the known past positions her as a figure very much at odds with the actual work of historians. As described by the National Council on Public History, "Revisiting and often revising earlier interpretations is actually at the very core of what historians do. And that's because the *present* is continually changing. . . . This is inescapably a task of interpreting rather than simply collecting data." Lucy is a conservative construct of a keeper of the historical imaginary—an enthusiast for the minutiae of the past, a fetishist of notable personalities and accomplishments, but in no way willing to do the kind of questioning and interpretative work of an actual historian.

As the series progresses, the intrigues and plots that unfold become more complex—shifts in time revive individuals who have died, and one character begins to experience psychic visions of the future—further emphasizing the role of fate in dictating how history unfolds. In "The Salem Witch Hunt," for instance, now-psychic Jiya experiences a vision in which Rufus kills Judge Sewall. Rufus avoids this fate, but Sewall is promptly run over by a carriage instead. Unlike the rigid demands of time to adhere to the known in *11.22.63*, the forces of fate in *Timeless* seem to operate by a standard of "close enough." The series largely dismisses Lucy's concern about specific details in favor of broad strokes: a government agent sternly instructs her to "take the win" when she protests that their interference altered the events of April 14, 1865; Lincoln was still assassinated, after all, and the other figures targeted in the conspiracy were not. This cavalier attitude toward the finer points of the past—the details matter only to those select individuals, like Lucy, who are obsessed with them—reinforces a strongly presentist ideology threading through the American historical imaginary. While big events and big moments are vital, the contexts and details are portrayed as the specialized purview of historians, whose knowledge may be impressive but is largely irrelevant.

Making History and Legends of Tomorrow

Not all the recent time travel series have treated the question of how shifts in the past may impact the present with the tragedy and drama of *11.22.63* and *Timeless*. Here, I briefly consider two series that use time travel primarily as a comedic device—*Making History*, which ran for one season on Fox in 2017, and *Legends of Tomorrow*, an ongoing CW series that premiered in 2016. Neither of these shows demonstrates much investment in the idea of historical accuracy (*Legends of Tomorrow*, as I will discuss, is particularly over-the-top), but their engagements with the historical imaginary are still useful to examine, as they illustrate the pervasiveness of the presentism that ultimately portrays too much interest in the past as detrimental that has dominated recent time travel narratives.

Making History centers on a facilities manager at a Massachusetts college, Daniel, who regularly travels to 1775, where he is popular with locals and in love with a woman named Deborah. He frequently quotes popular movies and songs to the colonists, who admire him for this as well as for his good hygiene. Daniel eventually realizes that he has somehow prevented the beginning of the American Revolution, and convinces Chris, a history professor, to travel back to 1775 with him to fix it. Deborah chooses to come to the present day with them, and after setting history right, they continue to make use of time travel for goals as varied as attempting to aid Chris's academic career to allowing Deborah to buy an ice cream shop.

Part of what sets *Making History* apart from *11.22.63* and *Timeless*, beyond their different tones, is how *Making History* treats the past as dramatically foreign from the present. While Daniel's easygoing nature and familiarity with 1775 allow him to transition into that space fairly easily, Chris has a very difficult time adjusting to the past. Upon arriving in 1775, he immediately vomits due to the horrible smell that permeates the town (Daniel offhandedly apologizes, saying "the past smells like poop because there is doody everywhere"). No other show deals directly with the visceral physical experience of traveling between times. Chris, who is Black, is constantly irritated by the immaturity and racism of the colonists; at one point tells a horse, "You get treated better than I do in this time." However, while *Making History* does portray the present as a more desirable space to inhabit than the past, it is not as optimistic as *Timeless* in its portrayal of contemporary race relations. At one point Deborah asks Daniel and Chris, "So, in 2016 white people and Black people are friends?" Chris answers, "Not at all," at the same moment that Daniel, who is white, says, "Absolutely." Daniel, despite his successes in time travel, is self-serving and somewhat buffoonish, and the show clearly intends to align with Chris's contempt for the idea that the status quo deserves applause simply for being an improvement on the horrors of the past. *Making History* is the only one of these series that gives some indication of continuity between past and present discrimination.

As in *11.22.63* and *Timeless*, *Making History*'s first episode includes a scene in which a teacher/soon to be time traveler lectures a class on what history truly is. Daniel enters Chris's classroom as Chris tells his students, "History isn't made by remarkable people. It's made by unremarkable people, doing remarkable things." The show then goes on to emphasize the extreme ordinariness of people in the past. While Chris believes his knowledge of the Founding Fathers will allow him to serve as an inspirational figure for them, he finds they are largely disappointing. When Chris tries to understand why Paul Revere did not take his famous "midnight ride," Revere asks morosely, "Do you have any idea what's going on in my life right now?" In this encounter and others, Chris is constantly dismayed by the immaturity and selfishness of the Founding Fathers he has long idealized. However, Chris's critiques of the colonists are positioned to serve as a critique of contemporary American discourse as well. In his attempt to repair the timeline and spark the beginning of the Revolutionary War, Chris initially tries to motivate the colonists with high-minded rhetoric about liberty and self-determination. He fails, however, and ultimately he instead rallies them to action by convincing them the British are going to confiscate their guns, which is both immediately effective and a clear critique of the priorities within contemporary American discourse.

Unlike the other shows examined here, *Legends of Tomorrow* does not center on a teacher who travels through time. It is a superhero series, which features a variety of supporting characters from other CW superhero shows as they travel through time. Each season has shifted its focus somewhat; the third season follows the team's attempts to remove anomalies (many of which they may be responsible for) from the timeline as they serve as guardians of history. While the plot is ultimately too convoluted to usefully untangle here, and features many elements of the comic book genre other than time travel, I want to focus specifically on scenes from the season 3 episode "Guest Starring John Noble," which provides an opportunity to examine how very recent history is being shaped in the historical imaginary.

The episode begins with the team dispatching members to Occidental College in 1979, to save a young Barack Obama from attack by a psychic gorilla. In the brief scene of his confrontation with Gorilla Grodd, the young Obama shows overconfidence in his ability to reason with a determinedly unreasonable foe. Cornered, he takes a deep breath and then says, "I can see you have some grievances, but perhaps we can look for common ground." The gorilla seizes him by the throat and responds, "It's time to make America Grodd again!" The team intervenes at this point, and Obama escapes, indicating the moment is simply a brief joke. Later in the episode, however, team leader Sarah faces a difficult decision and announces she is leaving. When asked where she is going, Sarah responds, "To go talk to someone who can think straight when the whole world has gone crazy," and the scene immediately cuts to Obama sitting in his dorm room.

The actor playing college student Obama in this episode is skilled at capturing the former president's cadence and voice without it sounding like an imitation, and even at this early point in his life he provides exactly the insight Sarah needs. He summarizes the problems Sarah has faced, advises her to be patient with her girlfriend (who is dealing with the revelation that she is a clone), and consider an "unorthodox approach," in combating the demon the team faces. While some of this ease is no doubt a wink directed at the audience about the ridiculousness of the show's plot, it also speaks to how Obama himself is being shaped as a character in the historical imaginary—cool, wise, and self-possessed. Even as a college student in the 1970s, confronted with a time-traveling lesbian assassin who needs advice on how to defeat a literal demon, Obama is measured, reliable, and compassionate. At the end of their conversation, Sarah tells Obama, "I really miss you."

"Guest Starring John Noble," is the only episode examined here that came out after the 2016 election. While the characters are still focused on maintaining the timeline, there is also an idealization of Barack Obama, a figure so contemporary that his presence in a time travel series is surprising. Sarah does not need an expert in the era to help her talk to the former/future president because they are from the same historical moment. Time travel here is used to facilitate the calm and reassurance of the very recent past.

Conclusion

The time travel series examined here all mediate an encounter between a representative of the present and a significant moment—or, as in *Timeless*, many moments—in the historical imaginary. These encounters largely push back against the highly nostalgic and idealized views of the past depicted in the 1980s surge of time travel movies in favor of a presentist view that does not entirely ignore wrongs of the past but dismisses them as necessary steps toward reaching the existing present moment—which is always the past's best possible outcome. Through these series the historical imaginary uses mass media to make history more palatable to engage with, but more importantly it provides an ethical rationalization for ignoring the wrongs of the past. The logic presented is that since what is done is done and happened as it needed to, there is little value in looking back. These series' focus on fate and their marked consistency in needing an educator to serve as time traveler provide ways in which to alleviate everyday individuals of responsibility for their historical moment. History, as shown here, is always out of our hands and best left to the professionals.

3

American History in Walt Disney World's Magic Kingdom

•••••••••••••••••••••

One of the most influential producers of mass media shaping the historical imaginary today is the Walt Disney Corporation. Disney films and products are a pervasive aspect of American childhood; Christopher Bell refers to Disney as having achieved "one hundred percent penetration in our society. Every single person has been exposed to Disney." The omnipresence and effectiveness of Disney storytelling as a force for reifying and reaffirming hegemonic ideology have been examined and bemoaned at length over the years. However, while the content and ideology of Disney's films have been examined, comparatively little attention has been paid to the ways in which storytelling occurs in the physical space of the company's theme parks, in spite of their extreme popularity and profitability. Globally, Disney's parks represent nearly a third of the company's revenue and attract well over 100 million visitors each year. In this chapter I will examine how the historical imaginary is narrativized for the customers as they move through the history-themed areas of the Magic Kingdom of the Walt Disney World resort in Florida and will consider the ways in which Disney positions customers to understand their relation to the past.

I choose to focus on the Magic Kingdom because, in addition to its being the most visited theme park in the world, Disney's Florida location is the space in which the company faces the fewest limitations on its desired shape, expansion, and presentation due to the corporation's ownership of huge expanses of land surrounding the resort and its extreme influence in state politics. When Disney first purchased property in Florida in 1967, the company was permitted to form its own political jurisdiction—the Reedy Creek Improvement District. The Disney Company is thus largely autonomous; it is not subject to potential local regulations and is able to act as its own county government. The company also influences Florida policy due to its importance to tourism and employment, and because of active lobbying of state lawmakers, who generally act to protect Disney's interest. Disney's representatives weigh in on wide-ranging issues, from "employee wage and benefit issues, worker's compensation, and changes in the Tax Code" to "water conservation rules, which might affect the company's 27,000 acres in Central Florida, or even minutiae about legal process in the event a document server might seize on an opportunity to serve Disney guests on resort property" (Liston). As such, the Magic Kingdom represents the Disney Company's vision for its parks largely unfettered by outside regulation.

Walt Disney World's Magic Kingdom is divided into six themed "lands": Main Street, U.S.A., a collection of shops and restaurants designed to re-create an early twentieth-century American town; Adventureland, which evokes fantasies of exploration via attractions like Jungle Cruise, and Pirates of the Caribbean; Frontierland, which promises adventure in the mold of the nineteenth-century American frontier; Liberty Square, which is themed around eighteenth-century colonial America; Fantasyland, the park's best-known section, which is largely dedicated to re-creating Disney versions of traditional European fairy tales; and Tomorrowland, which offers a vision of the future as imagined in the late 1950s and early 1960s. Each of these spaces is, in some way, in dialogue with the past and popular histories. This chapter will examine the lands that are in direct engagement with the historical imaginary's understanding of American history: Main Street, U.S.A.; Liberty Square; and Frontierland.

Disney's attractions are a mix of performances and rides, offering a wide range of intensity in terms of both physical experience (from sitting motionlessly in a darkened theater to enjoying the thrills of a roller coaster) and interactivity (from completely automated animatronics to devices that respond to an individual customer's activation). Despite this range of available experiences, however, all these modes of reception work together to narrativize an understanding of the past as inert and valorize passivity in our own relation to history. Throughout the American history–themed areas of the Magic Kingdom, narratives of melodrama and nostalgia are continually and cyclically offered as justification of each other to create an experience of the past as a space of innocence that every individual longs to be transported to. These narratives work to shape a space in which the visitor's experience of the park is used to confirm a utopian version of history that erases difference and struggle in service of supporting a unified national identity.

The series of theme parks and resort properties that constitute Walt Disney World are a considerable departure from Walt Disney's conception of what was initially referred to within the company as "The Florida Project." While the Magic Kingdom—a larger and improved version of Disneyland—and accompanying hotels were always part of the plan, Walt Disney's primary interest was in constructing EPCOT, the Experimental Prototypical Community of Tomorrow. In this "city of the future," residents and innovators "would bring together the latest systems and technologies to demonstrate the imagination of American free enterprise. Visitors from around the world would come watch how people worked, lived, and played at EPCOT, and then take what they had learned back home to help solve problems in their own cities" (Koenig 14). This is in marked contrast to Walt Disney's original intention for the Disneyland park in California, which he conceived of as a "kiddieland" called Walt Disney's America, where children would "learn something about their heritage" in addition to being entertained (Broggie 192). Walt Disney and his brother and business partner, Roy Disney, were both dismayed by the "disorganized urban sprawl" (Koenig 19) that had grown up around their California property, and the ability to dictate all that could be seen and built within view of the Florida park appealed to both men. But Walt Disney considered the Magic Kingdom to be the least interesting element of the project; he had already designed a theme park and was much more invested in what he saw as the potential for meaningful and continuous innovation of daily life in EPCOT.

Walt Disney's death in December 1966, after the company had secured its land in Florida and begun to cultivate corporate sponsors for its planned attractions and showcases but before construction had begun, permanently ended the EPCOT project he had intended. Roy Disney, whose reputation was that of the fiscally cautious pragmatist, in contrast to his brother's visionary dreamer, "insisted that the Magic Kingdom be as faithful as possible to the proven layout of Disneyland, incorporating only suggestions that Walt had earmarked for improvement in Anaheim or that would take better advantage of Disney World's unique climate and ample acreage" (Koenig 45). A second theme park, named EPCOT, was added to the Walt Disney World resort property in 1982, but this "permanent World's Fair" (Epcot Origins), with its precarious balance between retro-futurist nostalgia and technological showcase, is a far departure from the inhabited city Walt Disney intended. The later failure of the Disney Corporation–built town, Celebration (Campbell-Dollaghan), indicates that Roy Disney may well have been correct about the feasibility of his brother's vision for EPCOT. But, for better or worse, the redirecting of corporate focus from constructing a utopian future to securing a perfected past and continuing the original intent of Disneyland to blend entertainment and education permeates the ambience of the Magic Kingdom.

FIGURE 5 Map of the Magic Kingdom. (Credit: Accessed from the Walt Disney World website.)

The lands of the Magic Kingdom border on and blend into each other, but they may also be accessed directly by way of the park's central Hub, a circular space in front of Cinderella's Castle with a path leading to each land. Karal Ann Marling argues that the organization of the park's lands around the Hub indicates the influence of the logics of television on the physical space of the amusement park: "Like a Wednesday-night viewer [of the *Disneyland* series] the tourist standing in the Hub at Disneyland was presented with a whole range of possibilities. Like an impatient viewer in front of the set, the tourist could switch from one channel [or] Land to another in just a few steps" (74).

The logic of television may also be seen in the way the lands of the Magic Kingdom make use of flow, as defined by Raymond Williams and discussed in the previous chapter. It is through the creation of flow that visitors who choose to move directly from one land to another once within the park (rather than making use of the channel-changing shortcut of the Hub) experience the transitions as smooth rather than jarring, and the ways in which Disney's numerous gift shops (which are present at, but not limited to, the exit of every ride) are integrated into the experience of the park. In his examination of the ride Splash Mountain, Jason Isaac Mauro argues that Disney's popularity is largely rooted in the fact that "Disney provides for each of its rides a narrative frame. . . . The narrative net in which we are caught at the bottom of a precipitous fall matters. The story determines and structures who we are" (114). I agree with Mauro's description of both the power and the attraction of narrative embedded within the Magic Kingdom's rides. However, to form an understanding of how Disney World uses flow to create a cohesive narrative of the historical imaginary, it is essential to expand this understanding beyond individual rides, to include the experience of the park as a whole. Because the Magic Kingdom was (and continues to be) very consciously designed as one continuous experience, it is necessary to consider it as a unified space rather than a collection of discrete rides, shops, and performances. As Marty Sklar notes in "The Artist as Imagineer," "The continuity of Disney theme-park design is clearly one of its greatest strengths" (15).

Disney parks are well known for being extensively designed and controlled; in *Walt Disney Imagineering*, the park's designers describe the ways in which "everything Guests see, hear, feel, touch, smell, taste is considered 'onstage.' . . . The overall experience is one that is both physical and emotional, as subtle sensory cues work within large, designed environments to heighten reality and involve the Guests" (The Imagineers 30). However, the park is not reliant on maintaining the illusions of the space in order to be effective. Numerous guidebooks published by Disney, ticketed, behind-the-scenes tours for customers, and promotional videos are available to reveal the park's "secrets" to anyone who desires to know more about the "backstage" functions. The Imagineers (the company's preferred term for members of the parks' design teams), secret pathways, and rigorous protocols of Disney parks are thus also mythologized in their own ways, inoculating the Magic Kingdom against any attempts to puncture its illusions. As in any magic show, knowing that it is all fake does not make its effect on customers any less real.

Main Street, U.S.A.

The only entrance and exit for the Magic Kingdom is Main Street, U.S.A., and as such it is the first and last land that all park patrons encounter. An image of small-town America is thus the gateway to the magical fantasies of childhood innocence within the park. This resonates with a political discourse that has been in circulation since 2008, when Sarah Palin began referring to rural regions away from the coasts as "real America," in spite of the fact that the vast majority of Americans live in urban spaces (Smith). Both in contemporary political discourse and in the post–white flight moment in which the Magic Kingdom was constructed, the rural space Main Street, U.S.A. valorizes is implicitly a space of racial exclusion—its fantasies are middle-class white fantasies presented as both universally beloved and universally accessible. The space is designed to "take you back to a turn-of-the century small town from Walt's boyhood" (The Imagineers, *The Imagineering Field Guide*, 20), though "it is more closely tied to his *memories* of Marceline, Missouri than the reality of what Marceline was at the time" (23). This description, from a Disney-published guide to behind-the-scenes "secrets" of the park's design, provides a useful case study in the ways mediation of the past and memory rapidly accumulate layers of complication in the Magic Kingdom. It is well known that, counter to the implication of sunny memories provided by "the Imagineers," Walt Disney had an extremely difficult childhood marked by poverty and grueling work. Rich Karlgaard argues that Disney's fondness for utopianism grew from a desire to escape his "Dickensian boyhood." The cheery "memories" of Marceline appear to spring not from Walt Disney the man but from the assumed backstory of the television-character version of himself he cultivated in series such as *Walt Disney's Disneyland* and *Walt Disney Presents*. Marty Sklar, one of the original members of the creative team behind Disney theme parks, recounted how Walt Disney told him, "I'm not 'Walt Disney' anymore. Disney is a thing, an attitude, an image in the eyes of the public. I've spent my whole career creating that image, and I'm a great believer in what Disney is. But it's not me, the person, anymore" (14). The memories of Main Street, U.S.A. are thus not the actual Walt Disney's memories, or any actual person's memories, but the presumed memories that the fictionalized "Uncle Walt" of television would have had. This illustrates the ways in which the past in the Magic Kingdom is always already mediated by mass culture representations—Disney World constantly treats well-known fictions as interchangeable with well-known histories.

The narrative theme of Main Street, U.S.A. is one of homecoming—the space is intended to represent a perfected version of any and every American town, standing ready to welcome its sons and daughters (which every customer is positioned as) into the fold. From the beginning, this theming marks the ways in which the narrative arcs of the Magic Kingdom are heavily racialized and classed—paradise here is an idyllic and prosperous small town at the beginning of the industrial age. Customers enter and exit the park near a train station, and Cinderella's Castle, which marks the end of Main Street, U.S.A., at the Hub and the entrance to Fantasyland, is visible at the end of the street. Main Street, U.S.A. offers a representation of a "home" that exists between the real world outside the park and the thrilling world of imagination within it. Its promise is one of pure reassurance and innocence, without the banalities of daily life or the anticipation or adrenaline that accompany theme park thrills.

Walt Disney World's Magic Kingdom is in many ways a space of extreme contradiction—it promises customers an experience that is simultaneously thrilling and reassuring, unique and infinitely reproducible, magical and predictable. Perhaps the greatest of these contradictions is found in its portrayal of American history, which may best be described as joyfully nostalgic. Nostalgia is an affective relation to temporality, one predicated on a longing for what lies in the past and can never be revisited. Janelle Wilson writes, "Nostalgia comes from the Greek word *nostos*, meaning 'return home,' and *algia*, meaning pain or longing. Hence, nostalgia literally means 'homesickness'" (21). However, the home of nostalgic longing is one that can never be reclaimed; the place itself may no longer exist, we may somehow be barred from it, or we ourselves may be so changed that returning would not provide the experience we so miss. Disney World and Disney products are designed to cultivate feelings of nostalgia in consumers; Jason Sperb argues that "Disney's phenomenal, largely self-generating, success in historical terms" lies in the company's acumen in creating "the plan to sell generational experiences, or more precisely, to sell the *always already nostalgic* experience of being a member of a particular kind of generation" (ix). But the spaces of the Magic Kingdom create nostalgia for the purposes of immediately satisfying it— rather than being left longing for a lost home, customers are presented with Main Street, U.S.A. as a perfected home where they may always return. There is a multilayered engagement with nostalgia here: nostalgia for the happy American past Main Street, U.S.A. purports to re-create, but also a nostalgia for the space and experience of Main Street, U.S.A. itself. Due to Disney's aggressive self-mythologizing—in television, home videos, books, and music—many individuals, particularly children, who have never visited Disney World still hold strong emotional attachments to it as a site infused with magic, innocence, and happiness. This is illustrated in the film *The Florida Project* (2017), which, in part, depicts the way in which impoverished children who live near Disney World but have never been still wish to imagine themselves there. Even adults who have never visited Disney World previously are presumed to recognize the nostalgic tug of Disney's particular brand of childhood, due to their encounters with Disney's ubiquitous mass media products (films, television series, books, etc.) in their own youth. In blurring nostalgia for an imagined past with nostalgia for Disney itself, the Magic Kingdom claims to fulfill what should be, by definition, impossible: the complete satisfaction of nostalgic longing.

One way in which Main Street, U.S.A. evokes the aesthetic of a welcoming home (which customers can either long to see for the first time or return to) is through the extensive use of forced perspective in its architecture (The Imagineers, *The Imagineering Field Guide* 24). Almost all the buildings of Main Street, U.S.A. are constructed with the first floor to scale, the second floor to five-eighths scale, and the third floor (if there is one) to one-half scale. This creates the impression that the buildings are taller than they are, but because the tops of the buildings are smaller than their bases, it avoids the impression that they are looming over or closing in on guests—the thoroughfare instead feels open and enlarged. The angle of the road itself and the scale of the build-ings (which are almost imperceptibly angled toward the Hub) are such that the street appears longer than it is when guests arrive—from the town hall entrance, Cinderella's Castle appears distant. However, when the view is reversed and customers are making their way to the exit, the distance appears shorter than it is. Disney's Imagineers are extremely attentive to color in designing the parks, to the extent that "each castle, sporting a palette that emphasizes fantasy, is custom-painted to match the interplay of sunlight and clouds of [Disney Park locations] Paris, Hong Kong, Orlando, Tokyo, or Anaheim" (The Imagineers, *Walt Disney Imagineering* 96). Small trees line the sidewalk at regular intervals, and planters with seasonal flowers hang from the lamp-posts. The smell of shortbread permeates the air, and the instrumental soundtrack loop piped through hidden speakers includes both recognizable classics like "Maple Leaf Rag" and "Alexander's Ragtime Band" and songs from Disney movies arranged in the style of the early twentieth century. The design of Main Street, U.S.A. is apparently so effectively reassuring, recogniz-able, and appealing that the space has been extensively studied in architec-ture, and formed the basis of design of facilities that provide care for individuals with Alzheimer's disease and other forms of memory loss (Montgomery). In these "dementia villages," residents and their families engage in "reminiscence therapy" by moving through spaces designed to appear nonthreatening and familiar, "providing the same intergenerational opportunities and sparks of joy that are a hallmark of the Disney theme parks" (Snelling).

While I am describing only the Main Street, U.S.A. of the Florida resort's Magic Kingdom, it is important to note that some version of Main Street, U.S.A. is the sole entry and exit point for all six Disney parks worldwide. In each case, customers enter near the "City Hall" (a guest relations and informa-tion office) and then walk down a thoroughfare that leads to a fairy-tale castle and the Hub, a circular, centrally located space from which each of the park's lands is accessible. Its global ubiquity is an indication of how essential Main Street, U.S.A. is to the particular fantasy Disney seeks to fulfill for its visitors. That fantasy is detailed in the song "I'm Walking Right Down the Middle of Main Street, U.S.A.," written by Stu Nunnery, which is featured in multiple *Disney SingAlong Songs* home videos and is performed in the Main Street Trol-ley Show in the Magic Kingdom. The song's lyrics begin with a fairly accurate, if fanciful, description of the title experience ("I hear the music playing / From the old-time ragtime band / I feel the whole place swaying / With people from across the land") but quickly moves to the strangely contradictory ("I know it's no illusion; it's a dream that's here to stay") and untrue ("No one's rush-ing; there's no big hurry" or "You're welcome anytime you have the mind to appear"). The song vacillates between describing Main Street, U.S.A. in terms of the utopian small town of the past it is meant to represent, and the entry into the ideal contemporary family vacation space Disney is marketed to be. It is presented as both a physical space and an ever-present state of mind.

The only "ride" available in Main Street, U.S.A. is the Walt Disney World Railroad, which is located immediately by the entrance. The trains move along a loop from Main Street, U.S.A. and through the more historically themed areas of Adventureland and Frontierland before passing through Fantasyland and Tomorrowland and returning to Main Street, U.S.A. Walt Disney World's official website describes the trains as "a blast from the past . . . four meticulously restored, working narrow-gauge trains you can ride, originally built between 1916 and 1928." This is a clear claim to object authenticity. The privileging of the railroad in Disney park mythology is in no small part due to Walt Disney's passionate interest in steam railroading—his backyard miniature railroad predated Disneyland and provided much of the original impetus for the creation of that theme park (Broggie). However, the railroad is a method of transportation particularly laden with meaning in American culture. As described by Vivian Sobchack in *Screening Space*, the railroad in American cinema is "both complex and richly paradoxical, yet they are also circumscribed in scope from movie to movie. The railroad is not merely its physical manifestation, it *is* progress and civilization. It threatens the openness and freedom of the west and individual enterprise, but it also promises the advantages of civilized life. . . . The ambiguity and paradox contained in the Western's image of the Iron Horse are as rich as are mixed feelings about civilization and progress" (67).

The aim or implied promise of the attractions of the Magic Kingdom is not to convince visitors that what they are experiencing is "real" but to create an absorbing fantasy that provides superior pleasures to those available in the constraints of the realities of daily life. However, the "realness" of the trains of the Walt Disney World railroad is indicative of how the narrative of the Magic Kingdom intervenes in the American historical imaginary by blurring the boundaries between what is perceived to be authentic versus fantastic. As Walt Disney originally intended in creating Disneyland, the Magic Kingdom is constantly working to teach customers the Disney version of their heritage— reaffirming the past as generally pleasant and serving a clear trajectory of progress. Incorporation of "real" artifacts or materials throughout the park works to undercut the protestations that the narrative of the Magic Kingdom is pure fantasy because, after all, it is constructed from authentic pieces. This is the same logic that Richard Handler and Eric Gable describe as governing colonial Williamsburg in *The New History in an Old Museum*: "Museums, it is assumed, amass real things, authentic objects; and their didactic, political, and moral work, as well as their cultural prestige, stems from the display of those items . . . both the museum and its critics share a commitments to 'the real' as embodied in authentic, old objects" (222). Throughout the Magic Kingdom,

Disney makes similar use of various objects' authenticity as a means of invoking pedagogical authority over a given narrative.

Both methods of movement through Main Street, U.S.A.—the train and the street itself—work to ease visitors into a mindset to accept the "magic" of the theme park's various spaces by traversing spaces that present themselves as trustworthy because of either the legitimacy of their materials, in the case of the railroad, or their fidelity to a certain ethos of American history. Disney Imagineers have described Main Street, U.S.A. as representing "'Disney Realism,' sort of Utopian in nature, where we carefully program out all the negative, unwanted elements and program in the positive elements. . . . This is what the real Main Street should have been like" (Wallace 35–36). Walt Disney World's official website highlights a utopian view of history in connection to almost every potential attraction of Main Street, U.S.A.: the piano player near Casey's Corner (a baseball-themed quick-service hot dog restaurant) will take you "back to the good ol' days"; the Citizens of Main Street performers "celebrate the good old days every day"; the Harmony Barber Shop is "charmingly old-fashioned"; with Main Street Vehicles, you can "travel back in time" to "next stop: Memory Lane"; the Plaza Ice Cream Parlor is "sweetly nostalgic"; and so on. However, despite this commitment to a meticulously re-created utopian past, Main Street, U.S.A. provides a much thinner facade than most Disney attractions. The illusion of an idealized Victorian street is only maintained for customers who remain in constant motion from the entrance of Main Street, U.S.A. to the Hub in front of Cinderella's Castle, a central space from which all of the park's lands are immediately accessible. Anyone who stops to peruse one of the many souvenir stores along the way will find that the theming within the stores is fairly half-hearted, and the same T-shirts, hats, and toys are available in the space of the "good old days" as in the stores of Disney Springs and other parks. Similarly, those who stop at the Main Street Bakery for a snack will find themselves transported not to a quaint local business of yore but to a Starbucks, with the ubiquitous chain's familiar menu, and the option to pay with the Starbucks app and use rewards points, just like in the Starbucks of everyday life.

The fact that Main Street, U.S.A.'s commitment to portraying a utopian space of history extends only as far as the entrance of many of its attractions further underscores Main Street, U.S.A. as a space of transition between the "real" and the "magical." Customers are within the Magic Kingdom, but only just, and the necessities and realities of the outside world (a favorite blended coffee on the way in, a souvenir on the way out) can be accessed and attended to at one's convenience. Main Street, U.S.A. is meant to be enjoyably different from customers' daily lives, but not disorienting. In *Happy City*, Charles Montgomery describes the way the design of Main Street, U.S.A. triggers positive feelings in customers: "Main Street U.S.A.'s evocative landmarks—quaint train station, city hall, distant Sleeping Beauty castle—instantly orient you to the landscape, reducing the anxiety you are hardwired to feel when you are unsure of your location in a complex environment. At the same time, those elements serve as emotional triggers. . . . Disney's references trigger memories that produce feelings of safety and calm—though these memories are just as likely to have been drawn from an invented past as from our own experiences" (160). Montgomery notes that Main Street, U.S.A. is designed to function like the setting of a movie rather than an actual street—it is the space where customers orient themselves to the narrative they are entering in the Magic Kingdom. Many of Disney's early Imagineers had backgrounds in film production, and the memories that serve as references for the nostalgia and happiness conjured on Main Street, U.S.A. are largely those of classical Hollywood cinema rather than any actually existing town.

Main Street, U.S.A. is designed to be what Linda Williams describes as "a home 'space of innocence'" in her examination of "mega-melodrama"—a space that "support[s] the belief that moral good is possible. Most often that good is located in a distant childhood, or even an imagined 'back in the day'" ("Mega-Melodrama!" 525). Main Street, U.S.A. represents the space of innocence in the narrative of Disney World, counterweighing the two worlds it bridges—the compromised and chaotic reality the Disney brothers wanted to keep at a distance when they purchased the expansive Florida property, and the world of thrills, adventures, and villains to be triumphed over in the park. It is the existence of goodness located in the space of innocence that, according to Williams, motivates the heroes of melodrama, and it is the joy and innocence promised in Main Street, U.S.A. that is offered to incentivize customers to enter the park and also drives its narrative. Visitors to the Magic Kingdom must pass through Main Street, U.S.A. to both enter and exit the park—it is thus both the beginning and the end point of the customer's "story" of the experience of the park. As in a melodrama with a happy ending, the Disney customer/protagonist begins and ends their adventure in the space of innocence. Henry Giroux argues that the idea of innocence is the primary ideology that defines all Disney products; he writes that "the Disney Company has become synonymous with a notion of innocence that aggressively rewrites the historical and collective identity of the American past" (45) and insists that "Disney's appeal to pristine innocence and high adventure is profoundly pedagogical in its attempt to produce specific knowledge, values, and desires" (48).

The ideology of innocence Giroux identifies is mobilized throughout the Magic Kingdom through a blending of nostalgia and melodrama. The two converge at the point where Disney's brand of nostalgia moves from cultural memory to personal identity. John Hench, a high-ranking employee of the Disney company for more than sixty years, described Main Street, U.S.A., saying,

"There's some nostalgia involved, of course. But nostalgia for what? There was never a main street like this one. But it reminds you of some things about yourself that you've forgotten about" (Montgomery 159). This idea of awakening the inner goodness, innocence, or childhood wonder of visitors through the experience of nostalgia allows Disney to valorize its customers as the heroes of the melodramatic narrative it constructs throughout the park. The Magic Kingdom's design positions customers to understand themselves as the protagonists of a story that begins with their journey through Main Street, U.S.A. and to then be carried along in the television-style flow of the park as that narrative unfolds. Williams argues that the purpose of melodrama is to make goodness legible through the noble suffering of its heroes; nostalgic longing for a space of innocence serves as the suffering that verifies the morality of Disney and its customers, whose goodness is rewarded in their experience of Disney's perfected version of the past.

Liberty Square

Liberty Square can be accessed via the central Hub, its boundary with Fantasyland, or its boundary with Frontierland. The land's theme is generally colonial America, particularly Philadelphia, but the depicted temporality and location are often somewhat slippery from attraction to attraction. The space blends a variety of architectural styles, including Dutch New Amsterdam, Williamsburg Georgian, "the flavor of New England," and the "rougher-hewn replicas of structures from the old Northwest Territory" (The Imagineers, *The Imagineering Field Guide* 67). Throughout the area, "authentic" building materials are used in attempts to further solidify the pedagogical authority of the space. Imagineer Bill Hoeslcher recalled that the rocks on either side of the bridge connecting Liberty Square to the Hub "were quarried about six miles from where Washington crossed the Delaware, and they were bought at a lot of expense. We could have gotten rocks in Kissimmee. But we wanted some significance there." Other "real" building materials in Liberty Square include "some of the slate stoops of those buildings [that] were actually bought in Philadelphia and were in place when our country was still going through its Revolutionary War and when they were signing the Declaration of Independence. All of the lights are of the period, too" (Koenig 57–58). The fact that these materials are "authentic" is not prominently advertised within the park but is readily available "behind-the-scenes" information to those customers inclined to read guidebooks or Disney-managed websites. As such, any customer who wishes to dig deeper into the accuracy of Disney's account will likely first encounter the museum logic of authentic materials being equated with accurate historical knowledge. In the design of Liberty Square, Disney seizes on disparate recognizable designs that connote "American history" and sutures them with seemingly random "real" materials of "significance" to create a section of theme park positioned as an all-encompassing space of American colonial history. That this results in design styles neighboring one another that would never be seen together in reality does not undercut Disney's claim to authority in teaching history because the point is not to thoroughly teach any one aspect of the past but to demonstrate mastery of its totality. By including recognizable elements of a number of historical moments, Disney posits is own history as complete, both without need of and impervious to intervention. Within Liberty Square, visitors are offered a view of the past that begins, at the Haunted Mansion, with the pre-Revolutionary Hudson River Valley and then moves forward chronologically and south geographically into the time of the writing of the Declaration of Independence in Philadelphia, then further forward chronologically and west geographically into Frontierland (The Imagineers, *The Imagineering Field Guide* 75).

The first attraction encountered by customers who access Liberty Square via the Hub at the end of Main Street, U.S.A. or via its boundary with Frontierland is not simply aesthetically themed around the colonial period but ostensibly dedicated to teaching American history. Visitors who access Liberty Square directly from the central Hub pass a plaque that establishes the area's setting: "Past this gateway stirs a new nation waiting to be born. Thirteen separate colonies have banded together to declare their independence from the bonds of tyranny. It is a time when silversmiths put away their tools and march to the drums of a revolution, a time when gentleman planters leave their farms to become generals, a time when tradesmen leave the safety of home to become heroes. Welcome to Liberty Square!" This text is very much in keeping with the kind of descriptions used to set the scene in "living history museums" such as colonial Williamsburg, but it is phrased in a way that highlights the kind of passivity in relation to history cultivated by the narrative flow of the Magic Kingdom. The phrasing on the plaque resonates with television previews of upcoming programs encouraging viewers to "stay tuned," except by ending with the hailing "welcome," it reminds customers to understand themselves as within the story. However, here they (and the colonists) may witness Revolutionary history without any of the conflict or challenge of revolution. In this phrasing, the United States comes into being of its own volition—it is a preordained "birth," overseen by Disney. Past the Sleepy Hollow Refreshments stand, which serves funnel cakes and waffle sandwiches, is a reproduction of Philadelphia's Independence Hall. This site houses attractions that purport to teach American history—inside is the Hall of Presidents, a combination museum, movie, and animatronic show that offers a fervently patriotic telling of American history and the office of the president. Between the Hall of Presidents and the Liberty Square Riverboat are two popular photo ops that further emphasize this as a space of colonial American history: a reproduction of the Liberty Bell (this is not the riverboat, but a replica of the bell in Philadelphia) accompanied by a sign offering a detailed description of the bell's uses from 1751 to 1846, and a replica pillory and stocks for guests to pose in.

In the Hall of Presidents, Disney works first to make overt use of authentic historical objects as a means to claim pedagogical credibility, and then works to interpellate customers into a view of American history wherein they, and the American people at large, look on passively as heroic presidents shape the course of the nation. The attraction is housed inside a building whose exterior is a re-creation of Philadelphia's Independence Hall. Inside, customers are offered a view of what Disney presents as the grand destiny awaiting the nation after its birth in the colonial era depicted in Liberty Square. Visitors who elect to view the Hall of Presidents first enter into what Disney's website describes as "an awe-inspiring grand rotunda," decorated with presidential portraits and display cases housing artifacts such as "George Washington's dental instruments and Abraham Lincoln's leather portfolio." As with the train, Disney highlights the authenticity of these objects, though here they are used as a claim to authority—presenting material objects of history in the familiar format of a museum allows Disney to position itself as an authority on the history being presented. As with the building materials of Liberty Square sourced from spaces connected with colonial history, these auratic objects are presented as validation of the authenticity of Disney's presentation of history. While the Hall of Presidents is designed to be engaging, it is clearly presented as a space for patriotic edification rather than whimsy. In spite of the museum-like design, the rotunda does not actually function like a museum but rather grows more and more crowded with visitors waiting for the next show. On busy days it quickly becomes too crowded to move through freely, and only those customers who happen to be positioned near a given artifact are likely to have the opportunity to engage with it.

Once customers are seated inside the theater, a blue curtain is slowly pulled back to reveal large screens bearing the seal of the president. As the curtain moves, a voice-over recording solemnly intones, "This program is dedicated to the memory of Walt Disney. In 1971, his love for America inspired the creation of the Hall of Presidents, a place to celebrate the optimism and goodwill he saw at the heart of the American story. Walt's vision was to honor the nation by honoring the American presidency." Here the attraction emphasizes Walt Disney's patriarchal role as the head of the Disney park "family" (he is setting out to both teach and comfort through this story), using that as a means of segueing into a view of the American president as a similarly benevolent patriarch. Walt Disney had initially been interested in creating a space similar to the Hall of Presidents in Disneyland, but he was unhappy with the technology available. The idea was one of the improvements to Disneyland's design that Roy Disney allowed to be brought forward in the design of the Magic

Kingdom, and it strategically connected with America's bicentennial. This dedication exaggerates Walt Disney's connection to the attraction as it was ultimately built (five years after his death) and obfuscates the Disney Corporation's actual relation to "the American story" at that time. The protests against and outrage toward the Vietnam War and student movements affected Disney parks directly when, in 1970, a yippie protest was staged in Disneyland. Members of the radical group scaled structures on Tom Sawyer Island, smoked marijuana, chanted in support of Ho Chi Minh and Charles Manson, and attempted to parade down Main Street, U.S.A. before fights broke out, large numbers of police were called in, and the park was closed five hours early (Hunt). The rigorous ideology presented in the Hall of Presidents is not so much a rebuke of civil unrest, protest, and dissent as a rewriting of American history in which such things simply do not exist.

The Hall of Presidents offers a "great man" version of American history through its presidents, each of whom, according to the feature, stands "at that fiery intersection where personal character meets the challenges of the times." The movie begins with a brief narration of the establishment of the office of the presidency in the Constitution, George Washington's surrender of power, the election of Abraham Lincoln, and the Civil War accompanied by portraits, newspaper illustrations, photographs, and video footage. At the point of the Gettysburg Address, the screen goes up, and an animatronic Lincoln rises from his chair to deliver the famous speech. The film does identify slavery as the cause of the Civil War but only acknowledges Lincoln's efforts in its result: "The war becomes a dividing passage in the American story. The president's own inner strength and depth of character change the course of history." The mode of address presents a version of the past in which, throughout America's history, individuals have passively sat and witnessed leadership of great presidents, through whom the preordained grandeur of the American story has unfolded. Sitting quietly in the darkened theater and listening attentively is valorized as the most appropriate way to experience the events of one's time, where we are encouraged through the logic of flow to remain passive consumers of history.

The screen returns, and the movie skips forward to the presidency of Theodore Roosevelt. He is presented as "a knight on a crusade" to right the injustices of working conditions and poverty in early twentieth-century industry. He is further extolled for elevating the role of America internationally and establishing the national parks system to preserve the American landscape. From Teddy Roosevelt the film jumps to Franklin D. Roosevelt, who "knows how to restore the faith of people paralyzed by the Great Depression." From Roosevelt and the end of World War II, the film quickly glosses the presidents following him up through Barack Obama in a brief montage of notable speeches and images of their eras. Perhaps the best illustration of the totality of the attraction's commitment to its narrative of the presidency as providing "a guiding vision that calls forth the best that America can be" is the photograph used to illustrate Lyndon B. Johnson's 1965 address to Congress, which shows Martin Luther King Jr. watching the speech on television. The moment did occur—according to aides who watched the speech with King, the only time they ever saw the civil rights icon cry was when Johnson said, "We shall overcome" (Caro). But decontextualized, it is wildly misleading, positioning Johnson as leading the movement for civil rights and King as a member of his audience, rather than King as having effectively pressured and persuaded Johnson in the lead-up to his support of civil rights legislation. As Wallace notes, "Corporate Walt's history is a top-down version. Popular political movements don't exist in this past. Rendering ordinary people invisible as makers of history hardly encourages visitors to believe they can make their own future" (48–49).

As the montage ends, the screen again rises to reveal animatronic figures of all forty-four presidents sitting and standing on the stage. Each is individually identified, then the figure of George Washington rises and speaks briefly on the importance of the oath of office. The animatronic figure of Donald Trump then recites the oath and discusses the promise of America's founding, the great leaders he shares the stage with, and his dedication to the American people. Every president since Bill Clinton has recorded a brief speech for his animatronic figure when the Hall of Presidents is updated after his election. However, there are a few notable differences between the framing of Donald Trump in his presentation and Barack Obama as the attraction existed before its 2017 refurbishment. In the earlier version, after Obama's animatronic representative recited the oath of office, he paused for a horn fanfare and an announcer intoning, "Ladies and gentlemen, President Barack Obama" (which often cued audience applause) before continuing his speech. By contrast, the animatronic of Donald Trump is never announced or trumpeted; the name "Donald Trump" is spoken only by Trump himself, during his oath of office, and there is no clear space for an applause break in support of the current president. At the end of Obama's remarks, a loud choral version of the final stanza of "America the Beautiful" played, while an image of the flag waved in the background. In the new version, Trump's animatronic does not have the last word in the way Obama's did—the narrator from the film instead offers further remarks on the "genius" of the "idea of the American presidency" before the image of the flag returns and a decidedly more subdued instrumental arrangement ends the show.

The differences between the presentation of Obama and Trump offer a contrast between Disney's handling of a presidency whose narrative can be shaped to fit within the ideological view of the presidency as occupied by great men driving a great nation forward and one who offers a much more challenging match. During the attraction's refurbishment, there were rumors that the animatronic of Trump would not be permitted to speak, as his rhetoric is so at odds with the theme of the attraction, and at least one petition gathered thousands of signatures demanding that Trump not speak in the new show (Bevil). While Disney ultimately chose not to break with the tradition established during Clinton's presidency of having the current president record remarks for the Hall of Presidents, the attraction does subtly de-emphasize Trump, in spite of the fact that Trump's slogan of "Make America Great Again," policies of deregulation, and view of American history demonstrated through statements such as "Our ancestors tamed a continent . . . we are not going to apologize for America" (Le Miere) would seem to be in keeping with the ideology of the park.

Much of instinct to distance the Hall of Presidents from Trump's presidency, however subtly, may be rooted in his combative persona. Disney's ideology is predicated on the total erasure of conflict; the point is to naturalize its position rather than to win an argument that may arise from the acknowledgment of other possibilities. Disney's portrayal of history, especially in spaces such as the Hall of Presidents, relies almost completely on myth as described by Roland Barthes in "Myth Today." According to Barthes, "Myth does not deny things, on the contrary, its function is to talk about them; simply, it purifies them, it makes them innocent, it gives them a natural and eternal justification, it gives them a clarity which is not that of an explanation but a statement of fact. If I *state the fact* . . . without explaining it, I am very near to finding that it is natural and *goes without saying*: I am reassured" (143). Undoubtedly, Trump's more outlandish controversies and scandals led to his downplaying in the Hall of Presidents. However, his presidency was also threatening to Disney's ideology of history because it could reveal it to be ideological. Disney's version of history is founded on the naturalizing of erasure. Customers are not meant to notice the ways in which its fantasies are white fantasies—that there are no indications of slavery in Liberty Square, segregation on Main Street, U.S.A., or Native Americans in Frontierland. Donald Trump's eagerness to make those kinds of erasures visible by valorizing them works against Disney's interest to create a completely deracialized and unified national identity in the historical imaginary. Trump is anathema to Disney ideology because of his quickness to court every controversy Disney works to deprogram from possible conversations.

The next available attraction is the Liberty Square Riverboat, which demonstrates how Disney draws on well-known fiction as a means of legitimizing its narratives, similarly to its use of authentic objects to legitimize its version of history. Unlike the trains discussed in the section on Main Street, U.S.A., the steamboat that visitors board here is not a restored artifact but a reproduction. The riverboat, *Liberty Belle*, is powered by a working steam engine but runs along an underwater track. The seventeen-minute ride circles Tom

Sawyer Island, and its narration serves as an illustration of how Disney intervenes in the historical imaginary by using the wide recognizability of famous historical fictions to bolster the claims to authority made by its depictions of the past. The slippery logic of Disney's version of history is that it is immediately recognizable because it is largely built from preexisting, mediated representations, and that recognizability then becomes evidence of its authenticity. The steamboat ride is accompanied by a prerecorded narration by an actor playing Mark Twain; the script mixes famous quotes from Twain, trivia about the mechanics of nineteenth-century riverboat travel, and fictionalized descriptions of the nearby attractions (e.g., "That's Chickapin Hill—or at least it used to be. Dam burst a few years back, and folks been callin' it 'Splash Mountain' ever since. Some have even taken to ridin' hollowed-out logs over the big falls").

In spite of the riverboat ride being based in Liberty Square, the primary focus of the its narration is on Frontierland—both its individual attractions and the narrative space linking them. However, the inclusion of the riverboat in Liberty Square helps to establish the ways in which both geography and temporality are muddled in the Magic Kingdom's depiction of the past. On the one hand, the narration of the Liberty Square Riverboat indicates that Frontierland and Liberty Square are neighboring towns that exist concurrently ("That river town we're passin' is Frontierland. A few years back, it was no more than a boomtown, carved out of the wilderness by a handful of settlers lookin' to start a new life"). However, the spaces of American history they are meant to depict are strikingly disparate—the eighteenth-century American colonies and the nineteenth-century frontier. The design of the lands suggests that customers are moving forward or backward in time, and across geography, depending on the path they choose. But these details function primarily as subtext, and so guests are also provided the option of experiencing them as simultaneous and coexisting; the past is as immediate or distant as customers choose to interpret. This supports Disney's positing of the space as representing a totalizing and impervious view of the past—every necessary element of history is readily available to customers, in whatever form they choose to experience it. While the Liberty Square Riverboat and, as I will examine next, the Haunted Mansion may not seem closely connected to the stated theme of colonial America, they do much of the work of setting the tone and establishing the logics of the space.

The final attraction in Liberty Square before the boundary with Fantasyland is the Haunted Mansion, which is what is known in the company's terms as a "dark ride," where customers are moved via some vehicle through various scenes and tableaux along an indoor track. The Haunted Mansion marks a further transition away from the patriotic theming that defines the areas of Liberty Square first encountered from the Hub, and it is separated from the land's other attractions by a considerable amount of space devoted to gift shops and quick-service restaurants. Positioned at the boundary of Liberty Square and Fantasyland, the ride sutures elements of both the historical (through its architecture, music, costuming of employees, and depictions of scenes such as a grand ball) and the fantastical (ghosts, optical illusions, and special effects) in order to serve as a transitional space between the two lands. Though the ride's scares are primarily intended to be humorous and are unlikely to frighten anyone other than the very young, the essential beats of its plot—that visitors find themselves trapped in a labyrinthine mansion haunted by 999 ghosts and eventually escape only to be followed out by "hitch-hiking ghosts"—is strikingly macabre for a space that promises to be "the happiest place on earth." In the preboarding area of the ride, the "Ghost Host" that narrates the attraction instructs visitors, "Consider this dismaying observation. This chamber has no windows and no doors, which offers you this chilling challenge: find a way out! Of course, there's always my way." At this point, the lights flash, and the figure of a hanging man becomes visible at the ceiling, accompanied by the sound of a woman's scream.

It is jarringly out of step with contemporary mainstream American sensibilities for a popular children's attraction to begin by instructing visitors to consider suicide. In his book on the attraction, Jason Surrell argues that Walt Disney's death, after the ride had already been being designed, debated, and redesigned among Disney Imagineers for ten years, resulted in the "loss of his 'final say' [which] had a serious effect on the Haunted Mansion." This led to the Haunted Mansion as a ride fractured by debate between designers who felt it should be genuinely frightening (led by animator and set designer Claude Coats) and those who believed it should be made silly (led by animator Marc Davis). As a result, "The first half of the show is all about the environment—a testament to Claude's experience as a background artist. It is more ominous and scarier, with nary a character in sight." Midway through the ride, however, the mood switches to one "less reliant on strong set design and filled to overflowing with Marc Davis' whimsical characters and sight gags" (*The Haunted Mansion* 28). It is in this half that the popular, bouncy theme song for the ride, "Grim Grinning Ghosts," can be heard. That the darkness of the first half goes largely uncommented on in discussions of Disney attractions is likely due to the ride's status as a "Disney classic." Nostalgia structures much in the way Disney portrays the past, and the park also strategically deploys nostalgia in propagating the popularity of its attractions and experiences; the Haunted Mansion has been at the Magic Kingdom since its opening, and many Disney customers are parents who visited as children and want to re-create their experience for their own children. While the Haunted Mansion was recently updated in some areas, most of the ride has remained unaltered in spite of many of the effects now appearing dated. The new features did not moderate the tone or acknowledge the ride's tie-in movie *The Haunted Mansion* (2003)—unlike the *Pirates of the Caribbean* film franchise, which was a massive financial success, *The Haunted Mansion* was a critical and commercial failure—but instead added interactive attractions to the ride's waiting area and incorporated digital effects into a few select rooms.

There is a version of the Haunted Mansion in every Magic Kingdom park around the world, and in each park it is positioned in a different land—in Disneyland, for instance, it is a part of New Orleans Square, and in Mystic Point in Hong Kong Disneyland. In each case, the idea of a foreboding mansion where guests are hosted and playfully threatened by the supernatural is adapted to the thematic needs of the individual park. The Haunted Mansion is a part of Liberty Square in Disney World because the park was opened a few years before America's bicentennial, and the Imagineer team wanted a section of the park that worked in synergy with that event—the Haunted Mansion was intended to work alongside the Hall of Presidents to support this colonial history–themed land. The Haunted Mansion works to establish the colonial setting of Liberty Square in its architecture:

> The final design incorporated a number of strong Gothic design elements typical of pre-Revolutionary New York's lower Hudson River Valley, including arches thrusting upward into the sky, large stone foundations and cornerstones, and the stone and brickwork common to the English Tudor style. This particular type of architecture is referred to as Perpendicular Style for its use of strong vertical lines, which enhances the sense that the Mansion is towering above you, tall and forbidding. . . . Claude Coats himself played with the scale and some of the ornamentation to make the Mansion appear even more sinister and foreboding. The Mansion's two wings seem almost clawlike in appearance, as though the house is looming over you, ready to attack. (Surrell, *The Haunted Mansion* 37)

The Haunted Mansion is the final attraction before Liberty Square transitions into Fantasyland, where the first rides available after the transition are "it's a small world," to one side, and Peter Pan's Flight, to the other. It is notable that the narrative of both attractions is significantly more connected to the "real world" than the majority of Fantasyland attractions. The "it's a small world" ride is described on Walt Disney World's website as "the happiest cruise that ever sailed," in which "almost 300 traditionally dressed, dimpled darling [children] from nearly every corner of the globe sing a simple song in their native language about universal harmony and dance." As such, its connection to the idea of "fantasy" is in its aggressive (even for Disney) utopianism rather than the more typical Fantasyland focus on wishes and magic. Peter Pan's Flight, based on the Disney movie adaptation of the J. M. Barrie story, depicts a flight over the magical space of Neverland, but it begins and ends in the mundane space of the Darling children's bedroom. Both of these attractions posit the rider as entering from and then returning to the real world; the space outside those rides is thus positioned as in contrast to the magic of Fantasyland's attractions. In the narrative of their experience of the Magic Kingdom, customers are exiting the land of imagination and moving into the land of the "real" past, while making use of the recognizability of narratives such as *Peter Pan* and Disney's depiction of it to continue legitimizing the authenticity of the customers' experience of the flow of their own story/adventure through the park.

Outside of these attractions, the first marker of transition into Fantasyland is a bend in the pathway. As visitors walk around that corner, the architecture on one side shifts from the red shingled roofs of colonial structures to the flags and multicolored stripes that dominate the rooftops of Fantasyland. To the other side, the first marker of Fantasyland is visible in the recently added Rapunzel Tower, which is not a ride or a shop but a popular photo opportunity and a landmark for the nearby restrooms. This further distances customers from the fairy tales of Fantasyland. Unlike other castles in that land, Rapunzel's Tower is always inaccessible—it stands in the distance as a backdrop. This close to Liberty Square, a magical princess's tower is necessarily out of reach.

For customers who choose to approach Liberty Square from Fantasyland, flow is effectively maintained in reverse as well. The Haunted Mansion is thematically consistent with "it's a small world" and Peter Pan's Flight, in that its internal narrative is also one in which visitors are taken from "reality" and moved through a fantastical space before arriving back where they began. However, the Haunted Mansion's story introduces an element of threat absent from Fantasyland. Unlike the attractions of Fantasyland, where customers are supposed to savor the supernatural as an escape from reality, the Haunted Mansion prepares visitors to appreciate the "real" as it is presented in Liberty Square by reframing the fantastical space as one from which to escape. Customers then encounter the Liberty Square Riverboat and Hall of Presidents as the space becomes more concerned with more straightforward pedagogy. They may then either cross back to the Hub via the bridge or else continue on to Frontierland.

Frontierland

The boundary between Liberty Square and Frontierland provides a smoother transition than the one between Fantasyland and Liberty Square. It is located between two restaurants: the Liberty Tree Tavern and the Diamond Horseshoe. Unlike the gradual thematic transition between Fantasyland and Liberty Square marked by the Haunted Mansion, both the Liberty Tree Tavern and the Diamond Horseshoe are fully committed to their respective land's theme. The Liberty Tree Tavern is modeled after a "stately colonial-style inn," serves foods mainly associated with Thanksgiving (e.g., turkey and stuffing), and consists of different dining rooms dedicated to commemorating Benjamin Franklin, Thomas Jefferson, John Paul Jones, Paul Revere, Betsy Ross, and George Washington. The Diamond Horseshoe is advertised as an "Old West music hall" serving frontier-themed foods such as cowboy beans and campfire brownies. Once customers cross into Frontierland, the background music shifts to instrumental arrangements of songs such as "The Yellow Rose of Texas" and "On Top of Old Smokey" performed on banjo, harmonica, and violin.

Like Liberty Square, Frontierland purports to create an all-encompassing view of a period of American history that stretches across temporality and geography by treating different times and spaces as concurrent. Frontierland is primarily themed around the idea of the Old West, which is reinforced by its description from the Liberty Square Riverboat as a boomtown transitioning into "a fine big city" in spite of still having "its share of footloose trappers, keelboaters, prospectors, and an Indian or two." The gift shops ("trading posts"), restaurants (the Diamond Horseshoe and Pecos Bill Tall Tale Inn and Café), and Big Thunder Mountain Railroad ride all adhere to that narrative. In his analysis of the Disneyland version of Frontierland, Richard Francaviglia notes that "both words *frontier* and *land* are inextricably tied to *ownership*, either geopolitical, individual, or both" and argues the space is best understood "as a material manifestation of Disney's—and, broadly speaking, America's—mental map of the national experience" (158; emphasis in original). Interspersed among the signifiers of the cinematic gold rush towns that form the basis of Frontierland are the raft to Tom Sawyer Island (set in antebellum Missouri), the Country Bear Jamboree (performing Appalachian-style music), and Splash Mountain (set in Georgia during Reconstruction, and soon to be redesigned in the mode of 1920s New Orleans). According to *The Imagineering Field Guide to the Magic Kingdom*, Frontierland is designed to evoke "the wooded frontier of Davy Crockett, the Southern banks of the Mighty Mississippi, recalling the world of Tom Sawyer, the Southwestern U.S. [and] the Great Gold Rush of 1849" (The Imagineers 52). The treatment of these as one amorphous space is, at least according to Disney, due to Walt Disney's "fondest memories of childhood" and the joy he took in various adventure stories. Unlike Liberty Square, Frontierland does not incorporate authentic materials but instead makes use of the complementary logic of the historical imaginary in which highly recognizable mass cultural historical fictions of the American past are remediated into a space of "real" history for customers to experience as historical knowledge.

There is no overt indication in Frontierland of any significant history of struggle or conflict in any of the regions it depicts; all are reduced to an interchangeable space signified by banjo music and funny accents, but without any acknowledgment of the genocide, poverty, and atrocities that shaped the culture of these regions. And although it is not surprising that a family-friendly amusement park that famously advertises itself as "the happiest place on earth" would want to steer clear of such histories, without them the narrative of American history presented is essentially incoherent—a space of adventure without a source of risk or conflict. The primary narrative of Frontierland is one of narrow escape—both Big Thunder Mountain Railroad and Splash Mountain feature fairly involved story lines in which the rider is on a perilous journey. Both of these attractions align the rider with a historically marginalized group, but they largely transform the source of danger from systems of oppression to the landscape.

Thunder Mountain is set in a recently repopulated mining town called Tumbleweed. According to the description of the ride on Walt Disney World's website, gold was discovered by prospectors in Tumbleweed in the 1850s, but the mines were eventually abandoned due to eerie, ghostly activity. Since then, new prospectors have resettled the area and begun blasting into the mountain again. But the hostile ghosts remain, and now the mines are collapsing. Riders on the Big Thunder Mountain Railroad are aligned with the oppressed miners, forced to work in unsafe conditions and kept impoverished by a greedy company—the story of the ride collapses gold prospectors into coal miners. The ride is a mild roller coaster, where customers board open-air cars fashioned to look like nineteenth-century steam engines and are secured with a lap bar. The train goes rapidly uphill and downhill and around corners through a set designed to resemble the red desert and rock formations made famous in the Westerns of John Ford. Riders can catch glimpses of animatronic animals such as possums, vultures, and (during the brief period the train speeds through the "mines,") bats. They catch a quick glimpse of silhouettes of miners who are ignoring the danger and drinking in a nearby saloon, and they are eventually returned to the loading/unloading area.

In 2013, the queue area of Big Thunder Mountain was updated with interactive features that draw on the ride's narrative of an active, but troubled, mine: an explosives magazine room, where visitors can set off an explosion effect within the ride; a foreman's stand, where customers can view humorous videos of miners at work (e.g., having a classic Looney Tunes–style reaction to being unexpectedly handed a stick of dynamite); and a ventilation room, where customers can verify the safety of the mine's air by checking on digital/animatronic birds. This expansion also further developed the backstory of the attraction—Big Thunder Mining Company is now owned by Barnabas T. Bullion, whose foreboding portrait is part of the queue's decor. As customers wind through the queue, waiting their turn to board the ride, they are confronted with signs indicating the miners face difficult or unfair conditions,

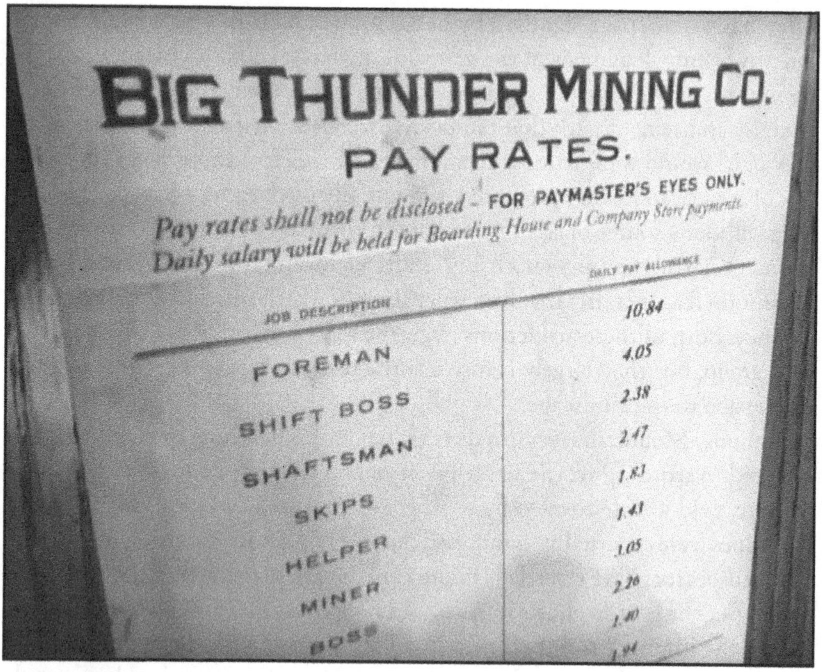

FIGURE 6 A list of unfair pay rates in the waiting area for the Big Thunder Mountain Railroad. (Credit: author's photo.)

such as "ALL MINERS are *required* to bunk on premises. . . . A fee has been deducted from your pay for services rendered plus gratuity" and "Miners are *required* to purchase mining equipment, clothing, and personal items from company store. . . . Fees deducted from earnings. All sales mandatory. All sales final."

However, all these elements are played for humor and fun. They serve to simultaneously nod toward the harrowing history of how miners have been treated and effectively erase it. These interactive comedy bits do provide, at the very least, some vague impression of the dangerous and oppressive conditions faced by nineteenth-century laborers, which for most Disney customers may well be new information. However, the cartoonish nature likely forecloses the sparking of any meaningful affective engagement in customers, and presenting it in a space of physical comfort (the air-conditioned queue), in anticipation of the joy of the ride and for comedic effect, transforms the traumatic into the whimsical. Of equal importance is that while the relation of bosses to workers in the mine provides the setting for the narrative, the "story" of Big Thunder Mountain is not one of challenging or overcoming the exploitative labor practices of the mining company but simply surviving a runaway train ride triggered by that company's disregard for worker safety. All the narrative elements of the setting introduced in the queue remain constant throughout the attraction—the adventure that visitors are encouraged to view themselves as the protagonists of is one of surviving a dangerous terrain, which acknowledges but does not engage with the fact that the landscape is made dangerous by the choices of powerful individuals. The roller coaster provides a different strategy for cultivating passivity in relation to history. Rather than the more typical address in which customers are encouraged to sit still and reverentially absorb Disney's telling of American history in the Hall of Presidents, on Thunder Mountain customers are presented with an indication of a harrowing history that could inspire discussions of resistance or struggle, but then instead are encouraged to trust the physical thrill of the roller coaster experience, where all ends well and all who enter the mines exit safe and a little giddy from a pleasant adrenaline rush (assuming they enjoy the thrills of a mild roller coaster). Consistent with the idea of flow, the only way through the story is to remain passive for it—to "ride it out."

Splash Mountain retells the animated portions of Disney's *Song of the South*, a film that has become so controversial for its aggressively cheery and caricatured depiction of former slaves on a Georgia plantation that it is no longer in distribution. In his discussion of the adaptation of the film into the ride, Michael Eisner evades the issue of the film's racism by saying, "We'd never release that on home video because you'd have to do so much explaining, historically, about the time it was made and the attitudes people had. But that doesn't negate the strong music, or the characters other than Uncle Remus" (Surrell, *The Disney Mountains* 83). As demonstrated at length by Jason Sperb in *Disney's Most Notorious Film*, every aspect of that claim is untrue—the film was immediately recognized as racially offensive at the time of its release in 1946, and Uncle Remus is far from the only troubling character. During the national anti-racism protests sparked by the killing of George Floyd in 2020, the Disney Corporation announced that Splash Mountain would be redesigned based on the company's sole animated feature starring a Black princess: *The Princess and the Frog*. How and whether that redesign addresses that film's setting of New Orleans during the time of Jim Crow remains to be seen, but the current design of Splash Mountain offers a demonstration of Disney effecting the erasure of controversy and conflict from American history and its own history simultaneously. By eliminating the narrative of the plainly racist live-action story line, it presents the history of the American South through another remediation of a preexisting popular fiction—in this case, the folkloric trickster Brer Rabbit. The log flume ride's story follows Disney's version of Brer Rabbit as he repeatedly outsmarts and escapes Brer Fox and Brer Bear's traps, finally manipulating them into throwing him over Splash Mountain (the ride's five-story drop) and into the briar patch that is his home. Splash Mountain attempts to elide the more troubling aspects of its source material—there is no mention or acknowledgment of the plantation setting or characters that made up the bulk of *Song of the South*. Instead, the characters and music from the film's animated segments, which depict folktales told by Uncle Remus, are given without their original context. The infamous "tar baby" that traps Brer Rabbit in the movie is replaced with a beehive on the ride, but otherwise the ride's narrative closely adheres to the film.

Sperb describes Splash Mountain as one of the ways in which Disney "strategically remediated" (198) *Song of the South*, removing objectionable material and refusing to engage with the racial discourses that have led to Disney's refusal to circulate the film. However, Sperb notes that the details in this new version of the story do not "avoid issues of race so much as they train their respective audiences *not to see racial difference* in any meaningful way" (199; emphasis in original). The attraction continues the ideological work of the Disney park at large—to render difference unrecognizable or meaningless in the service of a unified narrative of national identity. In Splash Mountain, antebellum or Reconstruction Georgia (using the time period established in the movie) becomes a completely deracialized space. The ride is populated with characters of traditional African America folklore (though they are in no way identified as such), and to that extent the rider is encouraged to identify with the culture of the disappeared character of Uncle Remus. However, there is no connection to the context of that originating culture—especially given Disney's obscuring of its movie adaptation, which serves as the bridge from folktales to amusement park ride. Guests ride on a log flume through a variety of scenes depicting Brer Rabbit, Brer Fox, Brer Bear, and a variety of cheerful animals singing songs such as "Pretty Good, Sure as You're Born." The log flume gradually climbs and experiences small drops on the way to its climactic drop, which is visible from a distance and the prime attraction of the ride.

Sperb notes that "it's difficult to 'read' Splash Mountain's retelling of *Song of the South*, since the ride is designed to completely, if momentarily, engulf the senses of the visitor" (182). The moment of the drop builds from the general anticipation of the ride, to nervousness or dread as the final drop approaches (animatronic vultures taunt riders with comments like "Bet you wish you could turn back!"), to exhilaration and relief as the drop is finished. The next scene shows the animals celebrating Brer Rabbit's final escape from Brer Fox and Brer Bear—dancers on a steamboat sing "Zip-A-Dee-Doo-Dah" under a sign that reads "Welcome Home, Brer Rabbit," before the scene progresses past Brer Rabbit relaxing outside his home in the briar patch, contentedly singing the same song. Disney combines the relief and happiness that accompany the physical thrill of the theme park ride with the song and imagery the company is most eager to preserve from *Song of the South*. Mauro argues that in this moment, "we are welcomed into the antebellum South. . . . We are relieved and grateful for this welcome, yet this overpowering relief overwrites and blinds us to the troubling and brutal implications of the narrative world into which we are ushered" (116). This is a different form of conflict erasure than that which occurs at Big Thunder Mountain—obscuring rather than rewriting as humorous—but it serves the same ideological purpose. Both rides transform historical periods marked by conflict and transition to static times of uncontested or untroubled power structures.

Conclusion

Whichever route through the Magic Kingdom customers use to structure the flow of their experience, the narrative ends with a return to Main Street, U.S.A. Moving away from Cinderella's Castle toward Town Hall and the train station works visually and spatially to signal the end of fantasy and a return to the "real world." In the Magic Kingdom's circular use of melodramatic logic, this is both the return to the lost space of innocence that indicates the triumphant end of the story (we have survived our adventures and, as good citizens who remained within the flow of the park, are rewarded with a happy ending) and the exiting from it that indicates the story's beginning (we are leaving the paradise of Main Street, U.S.A. behind and embarking on an unpredictable world). As the park's closing time approaches, Disney staff are positioned near the exit, waving and holding signs that bear friendly farewells such as "See you real soon," emphasizing the expectation that customers will experience nostalgic longing for the space until they return. If and when they do, the same circular logics will apply—upon entering Main Street, U.S.A., they will be both returning to the space of innocence (a happy ending to whatever their "adventure" has been since last leaving) and embarking from it into the park (an exciting beginning to a new melodramatic and valorizing narrative).

Undoubtedly, the counterargument to any critique of how history is presented in the Magic Kingdom is that the park is meant for entertainment rather than education, a sentiment that has been put forth frequently over the years. As Sperb notes, "The affect of nostalgia generates defenses just as passionately as do the feelings of joy and pleasure. Fans try to protect not only Disney, but their own memories" (212). People who go to Disney World, as hundreds of millions do every year, spend a great deal of money to go there and are likely motivated to defend the space and their experience of it. But this fallback, offered by Disney itself at points, is a dramatic oversimplification of what these spaces actually set out to do, and have done since first conceived of by Walt Disney. In some instances, such as the Hall of Presidents, Magic Kingdom attractions explicitly seek to be educational. Others, such as Big Thunder Mountain and Splash Mountain, are a presentation of aspects of American history that are ineluctably intertwined with poverty and exploitation that continue to have meaningful ramifications in the lives of many Americans today. However, the Magic Kingdom does not simply present

American history as wholesome, entertaining, and inspiring. It naturalizes the ideology of that history through the narratives visitors construct for themselves by navigating the physical space of the park.

Through Disney's mediation of mass culture, the historical imaginary and history are treated as interchangeable, and the park's constant and sometimes disorienting tendency to slide between the two while claiming authority to both illustrates the historical imaginary's most aggressive tendencies toward history. The journey from Main Street, U.S.A. through Liberty Square and Frontierland, and eventually back down Main Street, U.S.A. is one in which every detail—from the background music, to the smells, to the proportions of the buildings—is crafted to make visitors feel absorbed in the illusion of the idealized past; Disney's history is easier to buy in to when our own physical and affective experience seems to be verifying it. In this way, Disney's shaping of the historical imaginary through its theme parks may be more pervasive and difficult to contest than what is found in its movies and other media. Customers in the midst of the park are participants rather than merely viewers. Patrons are encouraged to either take pride in noble aspects of American history or view themselves as scrappy adventurers overcoming the challenges of its terrain. These two relations to the past, one of nostalgia the other wherein history is a melodrama and our reward for allowing ourselves to be carried along in the narrative flow Disney constructs is that we are its heroes, teach a very particular understanding of the past, and its ideology is one that insistently and damagingly recasts every aspect of American history as a necessary building block toward creating an idealized white fantasy given form with Main Street, U.S.A.

4

The European Legacy
and American Future in
Walt Disney World's
Magic Kingdom

•••••••••••••••••••••

In the previous chapter, I explained the variety of strategies Walt Disney World's Magic Kingdom uses to position itself as a pedagogical authority of the American historical imaginary and its consumers as that history's heroes. However, this focus on the American past accounts for only half of the park's themed "lands"; the remaining three spaces—Fantasyland, Adventureland, and Tomorrowland—engage with Western European history, the history of European colonization, and a retro-futuristic vision of an intergalactic utopia centered on midcentury American values. This chapter analyzes how, through these lands, Disney World positions the United States as the necessary successor to both European culture and European imperialism. Very few of the sites that provide as clear an insight into the logics of the American historical imaginary as Disney World does include an envisioned role of the United States within a larger global temporality. Rather than treating the United States as the totality of history, the Magic Kingdom provides both an imagined pre-America lineage and a post-nations future trajectory for the American historical imaginary. Examining these spaces provides a unique opportunity for clarifying how the United States is positioned on the global stage in the historical imaginary.

Adventureland

Adventureland can be accessed directly from the Hub or via Frontierland. The space is themed broadly on nineteenth-century adventure fiction aimed at young boys such as *The Swiss Family Robinson* (1812) and *Treasure Island* (1882). *The Imagineering Field Guide to the Magic Kingdom* describes the goal of the space as "look[ing] like adventure to *everyone*" and cites "the deep, dark jungles of Africa, the islands of the Caribbean Sea, the South Seas tropics, and an Arabian bazaar" (The Imagineers 38; emphasis in original) as the various settings Adventureland seeks to evoke. As a result of its exultant engagement with its source material, Adventureland serves as a monument to colonization. The connection between Adventureland and European colonization is not an act of thoughtlessness or a subtlety—it is an intentional and prominent design aspect. *The Imagineering Field Guide to the Magic Kingdom*, authored by an anonymous group of "Imagineers" who aided in the design and development of the theme park, note that the available transition from Main Street, U.S.A. to Adventureland (along the Hub) takes customers past the Crystal Palace—a Winnie the Pooh–themed restaurant whose "particularly Victorian edifice [serves] as the gateway to the Colonial-inspired visions of Africa and Asia that form the basis of Adventureland nearest the Hub" (39). In the Magic Kingdom, the pathway to the history of formerly colonized spaces is via the grandiosity of their imperial oppressors. The original Crystal Palace, from which the restaurant takes its name and some elements of its design, was built in London's Hyde Park as a venue for the Great Exhibition of 1851. This world's fair displayed artifacts and inventions from around the globe, but it particularly foregrounded the grandeur of Victorian England's power as bolstered by the resources of its colonies. Like the Great Exhibition, the Magic Kingdom presents spaces of colonization in terms of their natural resources, not their people. In the past as presented in Adventureland, colonized spaces provide potential danger and excitement to the "adventurer"/colonizer, but only because the land and environment are treacherous. There is very little representation of indigenous peoples in the colonized spaces of Adventureland, and those that do exist often demonstrate the impossibility of constructing a space of adventure for "everyone" while insisting on a cheery experience of European colonization.

For customers who follow the themed transition into Adventureland, the first attraction is the Swiss Family Robinson Treehouse, a re-creation of the set of the live-action Disney film *Swiss Family Robinson* (1960), which follows an early nineteenth-century Swiss family who are marooned on an unspecified island during a voyage from Sweden to New Guinea. The walk-through attraction treats the fictional Robinson home like a "living history" museum—customers are encouraged to "discover open-air rooms brimming with a bevy of 19th-century articles salvaged from the wreck" and to gaze at the living spaces

FIGURE 7 A corner of the colonial office space visible in the waiting area for the Jungle Cruise. (Credit: author's photo.)

of the Robinsons from behind a rope barrier much as they would at historic home re-creations in colonial Williamsburg or the Biltmore Estate. The museum logic of the lobby of the Hall of Presidents is applied with equal reverence to the props and set decoration of the artificial tree, which seeks to draw attention to the Robinsons' "resourcefulness in making a new life for themselves" (The Imagineers, *The Imagineering Field Guide* 42) on a conveniently uninhabited island.

The Swiss Family Robinson Treehouse is an illustration of how the Magic Kingdom places fictional depictions of the past, particularly those that originate in nineteenth-century literature, on equal footing with actual events in creating its account of the past. This tendency also arises in areas covered in the previous chapter, particularly Frontierland. It illustrates that within the ideology of Disney, there is no differentiation between reality and fiction— either is fair game as source material for the creation of an idealized sense of the past. Rather than negotiating the boundaries between historical imaginary, mass culture, and history, the Magic Kingdom collapses the three into an indistinguishable blur. It is a habit of representation that is difficult to pin down because of the constant slide between historical imaginary and history, where both are equally authorized as reliable via familiar representations in mass media and presentation modeled on the pedagogical ethos of museums. Fiction, particularly "classics" of American literature, may be of more use to Disney than actual history in establishing itself as an authority of the past, because the canon of American literature is far more stable than the narratives of American history. History is continually updated, reexplored, and rewritten by historians who read archives against the grain and reinsert excluded individuals and populations into the record. Beloved works of fiction of the past, by contrast, are much less likely to fall from favor than any individual historical narrative. By claiming mastery of both, Disney seizes the pedagogical authority of history while maintaining the defenses of tradition and imagination available to the canon of classic fiction.

Beyond the Swiss Family Robinson Treehouse is Adventureland's central plaza, which is anchored by the Magic Carpets of Aladdin—a "spinner" ride (similar to the more famous Dumbo the Flying Elephant ride in Fantasyland) where customers ride vehicles that resemble the carpets from the 1992 animated film. The design of the plaza area demonstrates how interchangeable Adventureland considers colonized spaces to be. While Liberty Square dramatically compresses pre-Revolutionary American history and geography, it still insists upon a temporal and spatial logic to the space (moving either forward or backward in time and north or south in geography depending on the direction customers choose between the Haunted Mansion and the Liberty Tree Tavern). In contrast, the Adventureland plaza is a round and therefore directionless space that seeks to represent all colonized cultures and times as existing simultaneously and as being effortlessly accessible from one another. The Adventureland plaza thus provides an all too on-the-nose representation of what Edward Said famously describes as the logic of Orientalism, which posits a fictionalized, undifferentiated understanding of "the East" as a tool of both colonization and identity creation for "the West." The actual spaces represented in Adventureland are, as Said describes in "Orientalism Once More," his 2004 reflection on the impact of his most famous work, "fundamentally, indeed radically fractious" (870) both in the time of colonization and in the present. However, he also bemoans the persistence of Orientalist beliefs in the United States, noting that "the hardening of attitudes, the tightening of the grip of demeaning generalization and triumphalist cliché, the dominance of crude power allied with simplistic contempt for dissenters and 'others'" has led to "innumerable histories and a dizzying variety of peoples, languages, experiences, and cultures, all . . . swept aside or ignored, relegated to the sand heap" (871). The disinterest in differentiating or recognizing Indigenous cultures, as well as the explicit approval and romanticization of colonialism that drives the attractions of Adventureland, is perhaps most apparent on the Jungle Cruise ride, which is accessible from the plaza around the Magic Carpets of Aladdin.

The Jungle Cruise has long been the subject of criticism due to its overtly racist depiction of Indigenous peoples of Africa and South America. In spite of these critiques, the ride remains popular and may well become more so, depending on the cultural impact of the 2021 live-action film starring Dwayne "The Rock" Johnson and Emily Blunt based on the ride. It is an open-air ride in which customers board boats whose design was inspired by *The African Queen* (1951) for a "10,000-mile cruise across Asia, Africa, and South America"

(Prieur) narrated by a Disney employee who acts as the "guide." The boarding area and boats of the Jungle Cruise are explicitly designed to evoke a British imperial outpost. A mixture of artifacts from conquered peoples and territories, such as tribal masks; cataloged insects; and an empty cage from which (according to its accompanying sign) a dangerous orangutan has escaped, are displayed alongside items that evoke early twentieth-century British colonizers, such as pith helmets, a teakettle, a vintage-style typewriter, and a pipe resting in an ashtray, to define the queue area as a working office of a colonized space offering pleasure cruises to American and European tourists. These tours are narrated by the Disney guide, who comedically explains and interacts with the animatronics and sets along the ride.

Most of these are depictions of animals (notably, *The Imagineering Field Guide to the Magic Kingdom* mentions only the animal animatronics). However, there are also multiple racist depictions of Indigenous peoples along the Jungle Cruise. These include the "head salesman," Trader Sam (shown with a top hat and umbrella, offering multiple shrunken heads to customers on the ride), as well as "a spear-wielding tribal war party [and] native dancers" (Mazza). As noted by Anne Zimmermann in an NPR interview, "The first time the boat encounters Indigenous people guests are told they're entering headhunter territory and that sometimes the natives attack crews" (Prieur). Throughout the Jungle Cruise, Indigenous peoples of three continents are treated interchangeably. There is no distinction made between locations and cultures, and all are depicted as either punch lines or threats—the same way the animatronic creatures that populate the ride are presented.

In January 2021, the Walt Disney Corporation announced the intention to change the ride to eliminate negative depictions of native peoples. Imagineer Chris Beatty maintained "this is not a re-envisioning of the entire attraction. It's the Jungle Cruise you know and love, with the skipper still leading the way, and at the same time we're addressing the negative depictions of 'natives'"; the renovated ride will "also have a cohesive storyline instead of just being a trip past a series of scenes along a river" (Mazza). The impact of these changes remains to be seen. However, the commitment to maintaining "the Jungle Cruise you know and love" inherently limits the potential for the ride to be meaningfully "more inclusive for guests" (Prieur). Even without the overtly racist depictions of Indigenous people, the Jungle Cruise treats the environments of three continents as essentially the same, with no need for clear distinction or transition between them. The removal of the current attraction's narrative of native people in colonized spaces is almost certain to be an improvement, but the depiction of these spaces as an uninhabited playground for the coded-as-white customers/"adventurers" maintains the same imperialist narrative of white European triumph over a hostile landscape as does the Swiss Family Robinson Treehouse.

The location of Adventureland in the Magic Kingdom emphasizes how this legacy of European colonialism has been integrated into the American historical imaginary. Adventureland is located between Liberty Square and Frontierland—two areas devoted to American history that are also directly implicated in colonialism and conquest. In all three lands, the customer is positioned to being in sympathy with or having admiration for the colonizing force and endangered by hostile forces of nature or the supernatural. The comical imperialism of the Jungle Cruise is very much of a kind with the thrills provided by unsafe mining conditions on Big Thunder Mountain Railroad. Both position past sites of colonialism's violent dispossession of Indigenous peoples as spaces of fun for customers who are meant to understand themselves as participating in that exploitation without inflicting harm.

Past the Adventureland central plaza, near the border with Frontierland, is Pirates of the Caribbean, a popular "dark ride" where customers ride on boats through various animatronic tableaux of pirate crews laying siege to, ransacking, and carousing around a colonial island. The attraction served as the basis of a 2003 film of the same name, which has since spawned four sequels. It is also arguably the Disney attraction that has received the most public attention and controversy for the way it has been changed over the years. As discussed in relation to the Haunted Mansion in the previous chapter, it is not usual for Disney to update attractions, particularly older ones, to integrate improved special effects or to replace out-of-date elements. While there are always Disney devotees who would prefer attractions remain static in service of nostalgia, these shifts do not tend to generate much in the way of broader discourse. The changes to Pirates of the Caribbean that have sparked backlash over the years are not those that attempt to bring the ride in alignment with the films, such as the integration of a number of animatronic figures of the films' breakout character, Jack Sparrow (Johnny Depp), into scenes throughout the ride. Instead, segments of the public (along with a few Imagineers) have raised objections to Disney's attempts to modify the ride in order to bring its depiction of women more in alignment with shifting social values.

When Walt Disney World first opened to the public, Pirates of the Caribbean had not been built, but construction on the attraction, a version of which already existed in Disneyland, began within a year. In the initial design process of the original Pirates of the Caribbean, Imagineer Marc Davis intended to root the attraction in historically accurate depictions of real-life pirates. As he delved into his research, however, he was disappointed to find that the history of the golden age of piracy bore little resemblance to his expectations. As quoted by Jason Surrell in *Pirates of the Caribbean: From the Magic Kingdom to the Movies*, Davis recollected, "It turns out there were very few battles with pirates at sea. Most pirates died of venereal disease that they got in bawdy houses in various coastal towns. I was sorry to read that because it took a lot of the glamour out of these characters" (24). Davis and his collaborator Claude Coats opted instead to base their pirates primarily on the cinematic depictions that influenced their own perceptions. Surrell cites the Disney live-action *Treasure Island* (1950) as well as on-screen depictions of pirates by actors such as Errol Flynn, Charles Laughton, Robert Newton, and Yul Brynner as direct influences on Francis Xavier Atencio's script for the attraction.

It is not especially groundbreaking to point out that Pirates of the Caribbean is a ride that took its inspiration from purely fictional films, went on to inspire fantasy films, and then was updated in ways inspired by those films. However, it is important to note that the attraction has always been fully and intentionally grounded straightforwardly in fiction in a way that is meant to be transparent to the customers. This only became more true with the inclusion of the highly recognizable characters of the film franchise. In spite of this, updates to the ride's scenes that attempted to de-emphasize or replace suggestions of sexual assault and human trafficking have met resistance from those who view them as "inauthentic" outgrowths of "political correctness" run amok.

The first of these changes concerned a scene of pirates chasing women, with presumably lustful intent. This was replaced at the direction of Imagineers Tony Baxter and Bob Baranick, who shifted the chases from pirates in pursuit of women to women armed with brooms and rolling pins chasing pirates and pirates pursuing women carrying trays of food—thus connoting the satisfaction of an entirely different appetite. Baxter and Baranick downplayed the degree to which the previous scene's objectification of its female characters and presentation of impending sexual assault for comedy informed the change. Instead, they pointed to the "decidedly underwhelming and largely static figures going round and round on turntables after the show-stopping animation of the two scenes that precede it" as necessitating the update. The change sparked numerous complaints from park customers and pundits who disapproved of the change and saw it as an unconscionable intrusion of political correctness into the ride's presentation of the past. Surrell notes that while the public complaints subsided, some hard feelings persisted "among the Imagineers who created the scene" and quotes Atencio as saying, "The show's called *Pirates* of the Caribbean, not *Boy Scouts* of the Caribbean" (99). In spite of the ride's commitment to the fantastic, many fans and Imagineers still believed its authenticity and, as a result, its enjoyability were tarnished by an attempt to reduce the suggestion of sexual assault as an element of its portrayal of piracy.

More recently, another of the ride's scenes centered on the exploitation of women's bodies has been revised. In its original version, the scene depicts captured women from the pillaged town being trafficked to the conquering pirates. A line of women, their hands bound and connected to one another, stand under a banner reading "AUCTION. Take a Wench for a Bride." The auctioneer tries to interest the pirates in a heavyset woman, apparently attempting to look winsome. The assembled pirates, however, are more interested in a sultry woman with bright red hair, striking fuchsia dress, and matching large, feather-adorned hat. As she plays with her hair with one hand and suggestively lifts her skirt with the other, the pirates enthusiastically chant, "We want the redhead!"

That the scene is straightforwardly one of sexual exploitation caused some consternation during the 1960s design process of the original Pirates of the Caribbean for Disneyland. Surrell quotes Imagineer Claude Coats as recollecting that Walt Disney "came in one time and even said, 'This will be all right, won't it?' . . . He was just a little doubtful of auctioning off the girls. Was that quite 'Disney' or not?" Apparently much of the concern lay in the redhead's brazen demonstration of sexual agency—it rendered the scene too legible as prostitution. Coats explains the issues with the scene were addressed through additions that emphasize both the unwillingness of the other women and that what they are being forced into is matrimony: "We added some other signs around, 'Buy a Bride' or something like that, that augmented the auction scene as though it was a big special event. Marc [Davis] had done other drawings of the other girls who were tied up and shivering. The way the girls were done, it's not an offensive scene at all" (32). The potential for offense, in this formulation, lay in the existence of an unmarried, sexually available woman and the implied rape of other unmarried women. This was overcome through the language of marriage. Spousal rape was not recognized as a crime in any state until 1975, and it was not until 1993 that it was illegal in all American states. Thus a marriage, even a forced one, was sufficient to make piratical predatory sexual practices palatable for the Disney parks.

In 2018, the scene underwent a fairly pronounced overhaul. The redhead has been redesigned from a prostitute (an interpretation confirmed by the briefly shown character "Scarlett" in the first *Pirates of the Caribbean* film) to a pirate. Her feathered hat has been replaced with a tricorn, her long dress and petticoats reimagined as a midlength dress with practical brown boots, and her hands now rest on the gun belt slung around her waist. Instead of auctioning women's bodies, she oversees captured aristocrats being forced to surrender their treasures, which now make up the contents of the auction she conducts. The character, now named Redd, is (as of February 2020) heavily represented in the ride's accompanying gift shop, indicating Disney's interest in promoting this change. Redd appears on T-shirts and keychains and as a collectible Funko POP! figure sold exclusively at the theme parks.

In spite of Disney's attempt to frame the change as necessary and empowering in the present day, fan reception has been decidedly mixed. As reported by Julie Pennell for *Today*, responses on Twitter included such statements as "Pirates of the Caribbean is a masterpiece. Yes, pirates did bad things and the ride depicts some of it. But it doesn't need to be censored." In an opinion piece for the *Washington Examiner*, Neil Dwyer bemoans, "Someone forgot to notify the folks at Disney's Adventureland that political correctness is out of style" and mocks Redd's redesign as a pirate with "#ShePersisted." These, and many similar, critiques all share the idea that the removal of women being trafficked and/or the portrayal of a woman as a member of a pirate crew is a form of fantasy too outlandish to be credible on a theme park ride about pirates that has gone on to form the foundation of a film franchise that includes apparitions, the kraken, human resurrection, and (apparently most fantastically) pirate women. Critics of the redesign ignore the fact that the original scene was *also* wildly ahistorical—pirates did not, as Marc Davis was unhappy to discover— engage in the kind of sea battle and city plunder depicted on the ride in the first place. If they had done so, the idea that they would then set up a mass marriage event that combined the worst elements of both human trafficking and Las Vegas quickie weddings strains credulity. However, this is reflective of the extent to which debates about the portrayals of the past in the historical imaginary are rooted in disagreements around contemporary ideology. The mid-1960s fantasy of a pirate bride auction is no more authentic to the past it purports to portray than the 2018 fantasy of a pirate woman holding a plunder auction, but the conservative impulse to lash out at the latter is indicative of a recognition of how contemporary American identity is mediated by understandings of the American (and pre-American) past.

Fantasyland

Directly across the Hub from Main Street, U.S.A. is Cinderella's Castle—the primary entry point to Fantasyland and the theme park's most widely recognized symbol. As discussed in the previous chapter, the design of the Magic Kingdom requires all customers to enter the park by Main Street, U.S.A.'s City Hall and move through Main Street, U.S.A. toward the castle as their path to the park's various lands and attractions. The symbolic spaces of power of an American everytown's City Hall and a Western European castle frame the entry and exit of every Magic Kingdom customer's experience of the park, creating an unmistakable resonance between the two. This decidedly unsubtle pairing of local executive authority in the United States with monarchical authority of medieval Europe emphasizes how strongly Disney World encourages its customers to view state power as benevolent, eternal, and unassailable.

Cinderella's Castle is a space of prestige within the park—a picture taken in front of the castle is the most in-demand souvenir image, and Disney photographers are positioned at regular intervals along Main Street, U.S.A. to take them. The restaurant within the castle, Cinderella's Royal Table, is both notoriously expensive and difficult to secure reservations for, as it is the park's "character dining" experience that incorporates almost all Disney princesses (with the noted exception of *Frozen*'s Anna and Elsa, who remain strategically limited to EPCOT). The castle also houses the "Bippidi Bobbidi Boutique," a Cinderella-themed makeover experience for children aged three to twelve that (depending on the package purchased) includes makeup, nail polish, face gems, jewelry, and princess dress, sash, or tutu.

Cinderella's Castle provides the entryway for Princess Fairytale Hall, a character meet-and-greet space where customers have the choice to meet either Cinderella and Elena of Avalor (Disney's first Hispanic princess, who appears exclusively in a Disney Jr. television series rather than a feature film) or Rapunzel (of *Tangled*) and Tiana (of *The Princess and the Frog*). Customers are admitted into the space with the costumed characters in small groups and are then permitted to chat individually with each princess for a brief time (approximately thirty to ninety seconds) before a Disney photographer takes a picture. The attraction's attendants introduce any children in a family group to the actress playing the princess by name, who then excitedly welcomes that child to the "kingdom." Children also receive their own titles when introduced to a princess, becoming Princess (Name) or Sir (Name).

The princesses typically begin making imagined plans with any children in the group based on what they judge their interests to be, with the aim of swiftly moving toward a cheerful family picture taken by a professional Disney photographer and available for purchase—either individually or as part of a souvenir package. In the case of my own group, "Elena" began by introducing herself and explaining the premise of the series centered on her adventures (though the princesses are not permitted to break character and acknowledge that television series or movies about them exist). When we indicated that meeting Elena was a major draw for the child in our group, she immediately pivoted, naming secondary characters from the series that my own two-and-a-half-year-old princess would soon need to be introduced to, and singing the chorus of one of the show's many songs with her. Rapunzel similarly picked up on my daughter's interest (given away, no doubt, by a brief period of bashfulness followed by increasingly forceful demands to be introduced to Rapunzel's animal sidekick, Pascal) and rattled off an imagined itinerary of royal activities the two of them and Pascal might get up to later, before coaxing everyone into position for the photographer. There is, of course, variation in the experience depending on the actress playing the princess and the level of enthusiasm of the child(ren) involved; Cinderella met our "princess's" indifference to her with her own clear lack of interest and quickly moved us through the perfunctory photograph, but Tiana gamely worked to win over the child in our group who had not seen *The Princess and the Frog*.

FIGURE 8 The author and her daughter meeting Rapunzel at Princess Fairytale Hall. (Credit: author's photo.)

In spite of this expected level of variation, Princess Fairytale Hall represents the Magic Kingdom's most direct and overt attempts at drawing customers (particularly children, though the experience is also available to adult customers without children) into their role within the park. As with many Magic Kingdom narratives, this role is one that must hold contradictions—customers are simultaneously royal and governed by the instructions of the Disney princesses; friends and peers of these princesses, but will not meet them again; reserved a special place of honor, but have waited in a potentially long and time-consuming line to claim it. However, these tensions are resolved in the souvenir image, the taking of which is the culmination of a princess visit. The image provides the customers of the Magic Kingdom with photographic evidence of their successful integration into the Disney fairy-tale fantasy without an indication of complicating factors. Long lines and the day's challenges (or, in my own case, a two-and-a-half-year-old child's outraged meltdown when the time came to leave the park and Rapunzel's promised adventures with Pascal had not come to pass) are not preserved in the image. But, more important, it is a Magic Kingdom image that promises a far more intimate experience than Disney can actually provide—it is one of the only spaces in the park where a souvenir picture does not include innumerable strangers wandering through the background or sharing space on a ride. Princess Fairytale Hall is effective at casting customers as characters within the park's fantastical narrative of their experience because it is crafted to create the sensation of the personal in the intrinsically impersonal space of the theme park.

Beyond Cinderella's Castle, Fantasyland—represents an amalgamation of geography and time. These include representations of sixteenth-century Germany (the *Snow White*–themed attraction, Seven Dwarfs Mine Train); eighteenth-century France (the *Beauty and the Beast*–themed area, as well as the Cinderella areas) and Denmark (Under the Sea—Journey of the Little Mermaid); nineteenth-century England (the Mad Tea Party of *Alice in Wonderland*); twentieth-century England (Peter Pan's Flight and The Many Adventures of Winnie the Pooh); attractions that are set either contemporarily or outside of temporality altogether (Mickey's PhilharMagic, Prince Charming Regal Carrousel, and "it's a small world"); and, most discordantly, a twentieth-century American circus (Dumbo the Flying Elephant and The Barnstormer). Unlike in Adventureland, this wide variety of locations and times are not presented as undifferentiated. During recent renovations, Imagineers have included additional barriers between new spaces, attempting to create more geographic and temporal consistency, particularly for new attractions. A *Beauty and the Beast*–themed section, which includes the Enchanted Tales with Belle attraction, the table-service Be Our Guest Restaurant, and the quick-service Gaston's Tavern, lies past partial stone walls that represent a gate and up an incline from many of the older Fantasyland attractions. Under the Sea—Journey of the Little Mermaid is farther out of view—up an additional path and blocked from the sight of most of Fantasyland by the Seven Dwarfs Mine Train. The circus pavilion, which borders Tomorrowland, has a gate over its entryway, indicating it is a discrete space more distinctly separate from the rest of Fantasyland.

While Adventureland presents colonial spaces as inherently threatening—untamed terrains sparsely populated by either ridiculous representations of Indigenous cultures or romanticized views of imperial figures, Fantasyland offers a hospitable and smiling European past. While a few rides do depict individual villains (Captain Hook appears on Peter Pan's Flight, Ursula is shown on Journey of the Little Mermaid, and the Evil Queen is part of the Seven Dwarfs Mine Train), they never menace the customers on the rides in the way the Indigenous peoples of the Jungle Cruise are described as doing, instead focusing on the other characters from the movies in which they appear. They are always shown to be defeated by the end of the attraction; there is no open-ended or ongoing threat in the European past as there is shown to be in that of the colonial spaces. While Adventureland is designed to emphasize it as a space of "otherness," Fantasyland represents the European past as particularly welcoming. In addition to the very personal interpellation of Princess Fairytale Hall, Fantasyland also includes Enchanted Tales with Belle, a larger group character meet and greet where children reenact part of Belle and the Beast's adventure together to the delight of a costumed princess, who then poses for photographs with them. Several rides are without any presentation of danger or tension. Enchanted Tales with Belle, Mad Tea Party, "it's a small world," Mickey's PhilharMagic, Prince Charming Regal Carrousel, Dumbo the Flying Elephant, and the Barnstormer all lack any form of threat or villainy; instead, everyone is simply enjoying uninterrupted joy at all times and is eager to welcome every new customer.

As evidenced by Main Street, U.S.A.'s role as the only path in and out of the park, as well as the attention to detail and "authenticity" in Liberty Square, the Magic Kingdom is driven by a view of the past as being filtered through American history. While Fantasyland makes no such attempt to root itself in "realism" or history, its position in the geography of the park indicates that this fantastical version of imperial Europe is a direct antecedent of American identity. The Americanizing of traditional European folktales and fairy tales is how the Disney company first found success. As John Wills writes, "Walt Disneyfied his European source material: simplifying narrative, adding new characters and creatures, introducing comedy and music, and highlighting the sentimentality." Wills goes on to note that something similar occurred in the early design of the theme parks: "While the homegrown Coney Island, with its tawdry look and criminal vices, depressed Walt Disney, European parks [such as Copenhagen's Tivoli Gardens] inspired him to create Disneyland" (54). The straight line formed by Main Street, U.S.A. between Town Hall and Cinderella's Castle represents the way Disney maps the relation in the American historical imaginary to European history— as a legacy of forward momentum toward the formation of the contemporary United States.

Tomorrowland

The only part of the Magic Kingdom not dedicated to depicting American history or its European and colonial heritage is Tomorrowland, an area ostensibly dedicated to imagining the future. However, its view of the future is one in which hegemonic midcentury American social values are unchallenged, unchanging, and eternal. *The Imagineering Field Guide to the Magic Kingdom* describes Tomorrowland as "a vision of the future rekindled from the past [that] carries with it a charm and sense of nostalgia that gives it a comforting appeal. Ours is a retro-future concept. . . . We all remember when we thought the future would be like this. Tomorrowland offers us the opportunity to visit it" (The Imagineers 109). In *Yesterday's Tomorrows*, Joseph Corn and Brian Horrigan describe these nostalgic imaginings of the future from the past as paleofutures. The objects of paleofuturism are simultaneously laden with the emotional meanings of multiple eras: the nostalgia and optimism of their initial creation, as well as the competing responses of cynicism, fascination, and (again) nostalgia of their reexamination. Like Main Street, U.S.A., Tomorrowland's affective appeal relies on customers' shared "memories" of something that never existed. If Main Street, U.S.A. is the American hometown "space of innocence" that, in the logic of Disney, should have been our national shared origin point, Tomorrowland is the promised future that would have been anticipated from there.

Tomorrowland embodies both the congenial and the conquest-based views of the past put forward in the other lands. Attractions like Walt Disney's Carousel of Progress and the Tomorrowland Transit Authority PeopleMover present the future as effortless, welcoming, and distinctly American; they essentially re-create the ethos of Main Street, U.S.A. across various temporalities. Others, such as Space Mountain and the Astro Orbiter, present outer space as the next hostile terrain to be conquered. These provide customers with the visceral thrills similar to those of Big Thunder Mountain Railroad or Splash Mountain, continuing the equation with danger, domination, and physical thrills that exists throughout the park. In "'The Future Is Truly in the Past': The Regressive Nostalgia of Tomorrowland," Tom Robson writes that as the customer moves through the Magic Kingdom, "time becomes impressionistic, with the modes and codes of one era informing another. . . . Disney's presentation of the future contains countless reverberations of Disney's presentation of the past. Disney's destruction of linear time thus encourages a fundamentally conservative view of the future" (25).

The reverberations across eras described by Robson are absolutely foundational to the presentation of the future in Tomorrowland, but the Magic Kingdom's relationship to linear time is not precisely destruction. Customers can and are encouraged to move through representations of varying times and spaces at will, but this freedom is always granted through the park's imbuing of itself with some particular form of pedagogical authority over the time period it has selected—examples discussed so far in this book include the sourcing of stones or presidential artifacts in Liberty Square, the work of Mark Twain in Frontierland, and nineteenth-century genre fiction in Adventureland. In each instance, linear time remains intact. Disney customers are authorized to traverse it, overcoming the limits of their temporality through the blessing of whatever framework, real or fictional, Disney has selected as the most appropriate one for understanding the past. However, in Tomorrowland the primary authority figure is Walt Disney himself.

In spite of his death before planning for the Magic Kingdom in Disney World had meaningfully begun, it is Walt Disney's own interest in envisioning particular forms of technologically enabled utopias that Tomorrowland cites as the source of its authority over the future. Janet Wasko points out that heavy mythologizing of Walt Disney, the person, has been an ongoing project for decades, begun by Disney himself. She writes that the fictionalized history of

Uncle Walt "was deliberately constructed by Walt Disney himself and carefully repeated over the years by Disney, his family, and the Disney company" (239), and that this "great man history" of Disney (and the corporation that bears his name) "benefits the company and will continue to be promoted as such" (244). In the space of the Magic Kingdom, the myth of Walt Disney is more than a benefit—it is an ideological foundation that rationalizes the park's view of both the past and the future, shaping our relation to temporality through the authority of the nation's patriarchs (particularly visible in the Hall of Presidents). The Magic Kingdom in general, but particularly Main Street, U.S.A. and Tomorrowland, requires a fictional version of Walt Disney through which to justify the park's authority over time. Main Street, U.S.A. is "Uncle Walt's" childhood, and Tomorrowland is the future he is always about to build for the nation.

This is most apparent in the Carousel of Progress, a twenty-minute animatronic show that follows a family through four generations across the twentieth century, and particularly the changing technological developments across that time. This is very much in keeping with the paleofutures examined by Corn and Horrigan, which "presume that material means can ameliorate social problems and even perfect society" (xii). A focus on the improvements brought by technology means that the future is "identified with consumerism . . . rather than improving relations between classes, nations, or races, or changing the distribution of wealth or standard of living—the future becomes strictly a matter of *things*" (11). In spite of its apparent focus on innovation and change, the attraction begins with a strong invocation of the past. An initial curtain rises to show a second curtain with the attraction's logo, and a voice-over describes the history of the Carousel of Progress to the audience. The tone with which the male speaker addresses the customers is familiar and casual. He promises, "Ah, you're in for a real treat," before explaining, "The Carousel of Progress was Walt's own idea from beginning to end. He loved it." He makes the dubious claim that "the Carousel of Progress has had more performances than any other stage show in the history of American theater," equating the attraction with live performances to which audiences choose to buy tickets, as opposed to a nearly continuously running theme park attraction that customers may wander into in search of air-conditioning and a comfortable chair and find to their dismay they are unable to leave until the "show" ends. Having established the attraction's dearness to "Uncle Walt" in terms very much in keeping with that persona, the voice-over makes a stumbling pivot toward patriotism: "You know, Walt loved the idea of progress, and he loved the American family. And he himself was probably as American as anyone could possibly be. He thought it would be fun to watch the American family go through the twentieth century, experiencing all the new wonders as they came." The linking of these apparently unconnected ideas—Walt Disney, his fondness for nuclear families of the United States, his unexplainedly unique patriotism, and his interest in progress—seems to transform enjoyment of the Carousel of Progress into a moral imperative. How could an audience fail to appreciate the unique gift bestowed on them by this unmatched patriarch of the American family?

The first scene is set in February "around the turn of the twentieth century," followed by a segment set in July "some twenty-odd years" later. The third segment takes place on Halloween in "the fabulous forties," and the final portion is set on Christmas in either the present or the near future. In each of the first three segments, the family father, sitting center stage and accompanied by his dog, directly addresses the audience. He explains what is happening in popular culture and what recent technological innovations the family is benefiting from. His wife and children make appearances on the left and right portions of the stage, commenting on or engaging with whatever piece of technology is currently relevant to them, and as the segment ends, the father sings the Sherman Brothers' song "There's a Great Big Beautiful Tomorrow" as the theater rotates and the audience is moved to the next temporal point of interest. In the final segment the stage is wider, and the family members are more evenly dispersed around the living room as they play virtual reality games and discuss the wonders of their various voice-commanded appliances. They all sing "There's a Great Big Beautiful Tomorrow" as the audience rotates away to the room from which they will exit.

In his critique of the attraction, Robson notes that "by presenting a world centered around a man as the center of the family unit, and without acknowledging significant contributions by women, people of color, queer people, or any conception of family without a cis-gendered, heterosexual, white man at its core, the Carousel of Progress simply reifies traditional values" (37). Indeed, the arc of the Carousel of Progress narrative takes the family imagined to inhabit Main Street, U.S.A. and projects it, unchanged, across more than a century. While the attraction is ostensibly focused on "progress," the family depicted remains in absolute stasis. Progress only comes from the acceleration of technological innovation and the perceived increases of convenience within a consumer culture. The family unit, where "women and young people . . . are quite literally relegated to the margins of the stage, while the center is held by a paternalistic figure and his trusty dog" (37), is entirely unchanged across the century except for their accessories. As described by Corn and Horrigan, paleo-futures are rooted in a belief that technology's ability to solve society's ills will lead to a return of values that felt lost, not a shift toward new one. Thus, "the history of the American future . . . is essentially a history of people attempting to project the values of the past and present into an idealized form. It is a history of conservative action in the guise of newness" (135). Looking forward is thus "at the same time, a nostalgic glance backward to a past of simplicity and 'common sense'" (4). The aggressively patriarchal, white family unit as the center of American life is the central ideology of the Carousel of Progress; after an almost unbearably tedious twenty minutes, the audience arrives, in true carousel fashion, back where they began to find that there were no significant changes made on this circular and repetitive journey.

While the Carousel of Progress makes a strong implicit connection between the past of Main Street, U.S.A. and the proposed future of Tomorrowland, the Tomorrowland Transit Authority PeopleMover resonates with another attraction—the *Liberty Belle* steamboat of Liberty Square. Both are presented as forms of public transportation that provide customers with a privileged viewpoint of their particular area. The PeopleMover, which the Disney World website describes as the "mass transit system of the future," is a series of slow-moving, open-air tram cars that run along an elevated track through and around several Tomorrowland attractions. The tracks also move through a few enclosed spaces that can only be accessed on the ride; however, these spaces show simple illustrations or stationary models and, with the exception of the model of Progress City at the ride's beginning, go uncommented on. Like the *Liberty Belle*, the PeopleMover is accompanied by a voice-over that provides the park's narrative of the space. On the PeopleMover, however, the narrator acts more as a tour guide, straightforwardly describing and encouraging customers to visit each attraction. The Carousel of Progress receives particular attention; the theme song is quoted both as the PeopleMover passes the carousel and again when the ride returns customers to the embarking point for their departure.

As the PeopleMover begins, it moves through an enclosed space that shows a small, illuminated model of a futuristic city. The voice-over rapidly rattles off the following description: "The Tomorrowland Transit Authority proudly presents Progress City, Walt Disney's dream for an experimental prototype community of tomorrow. Progress City was the inspiration for EPCOT. The meaning of its forward thinking ideas [has] been realized throughout Walt Disney World." This perfunctory invocation of Walt Disney's interest in technological utopianism functions similarly to the introductory voice-over of the Carousel of Progress. Once again, the Magic Kingdom's claim to authority over the future lies with its deceased founder's interest in long-since-outdated technologies. The model of Progress City here is deeply unimpressive by Disney World standards—on the scale and level of detail of a fairly nice model train set—and the voice-over script barely bothers to paper over how thoroughly Walt Disney's idea for the Experimental Prototype Community of Tomorrow was discarded after his death. There is no meaningful way in which the idea of a functioning, inhabited, technological utopian city has "been realized," or ever could be, through the attractions of ticketed amusement parks. But here the Magic Kingdom's tendency to blur fiction and history transforms an idea Walt Disney had but did not live to pursue into something he accomplished. Like the velvet ropes of the Swiss Family Robinson Treehouse, which turn a re-creation of a fictionalized set into a museum, the model of Progress City posits a future Disney World's customers may access because Walt Disney himself is always still in the process of building the version of his future that died with him in 1966.

Conclusion

In examining Adventureland, Fantasyland, and Tomorrowland, this chapter makes clear the ways in which the space of the Magic Kingdom collapse historical imaginary, mass media, and history into one another, creating a self-justifying understanding of American identity throughout a past defined by a heritage of European conquest and a future in which nostalgic values are perfected by increased consumerism. Taken in its entirety, the Magic Kingdom provides the clearest distillation of the American historical imaginary untempered by pressure for accuracy. By alternately drawing on well-known mass media and material artifacts in its presentation of the past, Disney paradoxically positions itself as an authority of both pure fantasy and historical accuracy without ever bothering to meaningfully distinguish the two. Given the Disney Corporation's dominance of the American media landscape, it is vital to understand its melding of the historical imaginary, mass media, and history if we ever hope to be able to meaningfully untangle them in American culture.

Quentin Tarantino's
Alternate Histories

•••••••••••••••••••••

In *Remaking History*, Jerome de Groot argues that the main critique of fiction-alized representations of the past—that they are inaccurate and incapable of providing rigorous historical knowledge—misses the point of what historical fictions do: "challenge, 'pervert,' critique, and queer a normative, straightfor-ward, linear, self-proscribing History . . . while suggesting instead a set of very strange templates for a type of understanding that does not neatly fit with per-ceived notions of the 'historical'" (2). De Groot calls for understanding his-torical fictions on their own terms, not as straightforward representations of what has occurred but as "modes of knowing the past" (3). In this, he is in keep-ing with other scholars interested in the depiction of the past through film and television, a field Mia Treacey argues should be termed "screened history." Robert Rosenstone, one of the foundational thinkers of screened history, sees the examination of historical film as a means of meaningful relation with the past as a vital path of inquiry (*Visions of the Past*), and Robert Burgoyne offers film's "ability to establish an emotional connection to the past, a connection that can awaken a powerful sense of national belonging or a probing sense of national self-scrutiny" (2), as an alternative to discussions of historical accuracy in *The Hollywood Historical Film*. This chapter builds on the body of theory established by Rosenstone, Burgoyne, and others who argue for the usefulness of screened history beyond a re-creation of past events judged by the exactness of their reproduction. As de Groot argues, screened histories contribute to the historical imaginary "both in their diegetic content and also in the modes of narrativization, knowing, and articulation that they deploy" (*Remaking History* 2).

This chapter examines the role of screened history in the historical imaginary through analysis of a vital but underexamined category of historical representation—those whose actions dramatically rupture from the accepted historical timeline. These works of alternate, or counterfactual, history diverge from audience expectations to form a unique engagement with both the past as it is shown on-screen and history as it has come to be known by more traditional means. In recent years, there has been a proliferation of such works; as Gavriel Rosenfeld writes in "Why Do We Ask 'What If?'": "So dramatic has the emergence of alternate history been that it has been reported on by the mass media and even grudgingly acknowledged by its most hostile critics—historians. . . . Alternate history has become a veritable phenomenon in contemporary Western culture" (90–91). Rosenfeld argues that alternate history is "inherently presentist. It explores the past less for its own sake than to utilize it instrumentally to comment upon the present" (92). Catherine Gallagher comes to a similar conclusion in her study of the alternate history novels *Bring the Jubilee* (1953) and *The Man in the High Castle* (1962): that such speculative novels remain popular because "they ask important questions—such as, are the American people [in the present] living according to the principles for which they fought?" (59). I argue that rather than being purely presentist, counterfactual depictions of the past provide a means of engaging the volatility of the present moment's relation to history. Because the departure from the facts is foregrounded in counterfactual histories, accepted discourses of the past are not erased even as they are written over; the contrast between the two historical narratives remains in constant tension through the experience of the simultaneously familiar and strange past. In this, I am taking up Burgoyne's description of the function of the historical film generally, which he argues "like the mythic figure of Janus, looks to both the past and the present" (11). This chapter analyzes the ways in which alternate screened histories intervene in the historical imaginary, and investigates the uses of such histories in augmenting historical knowledge.

I will examine the way in which counterfactual screened histories that depart from the accepted timeline intervene in the historical imaginary by analyzing three particularly prominent examples from writer-director Quentin Tarantino: *Inglourious Basterds* (2009), *Django Unchained* (2012), and *Once upon a Time . . . in Hollywood* (2019). While there is some overlap in the way these three films approach rewriting the past and what they attempt to indicate about the present, they are also distinct in which strategies of cinematic address they mobilize in their attempts to reconfigure history. I focus particularly on Tarantino's work because his engagement with the past is unique among major Hollywood productions; his historical films provide a distinct model of cinematic address of history that is legible to mainstream viewers while also challenging typical narratives that have dominated screened histories. Tarantino's engagements with history are often messy and consistently controversial, but their wide distribution and audience penetration, combined with Tarantino's status as a highly regarded auteur, means they are especially well positioned to have a sustained impact on the historical imaginary.

Inglourious Basterds

Tarantino's film *Inglourious Basterds* (2009) rescripts the end of World War II as a violent spectacle of Jewish revenge for Nazi atrocities. The title refers to a guerrilla unit consisting primarily of Jewish American soldiers who wage a campaign of terror and mayhem against Nazi soldiers in occupied France. The film is also the story of Shosanna Dreyfus, a French Jew who escapes the slaughter of her family and successfully hides her identity as a movie theater owner in Paris. When a Nazi war hero becomes smitten with Shosanna, he insists that the premiere of a movie based on his exploits be screened at her theater. Shosanna and the Basterds, each unaware of the existence of the other, separately resolve to blow up the theater and thus kill the entire Nazi high command at the premiere. Most of the film adheres to typical genre conventions of historical fiction—telling a story in which the audience is aware that the main characters are fictional but adhering to a widely accepted vision of the past enough to not challenge viewer expectations. Its final chapter, however, ruptures the accepted narrative of the historical imaginary, as the dual plans of sabotage unexpectedly succeed, trapping the Nazi high command in a cinema set ablaze by Shoshanna, as two of the Basterds armed with machine guns obliterate Adolf Hitler and Joseph Goebbels. By alternating between aesthetics of excess and realism throughout the film, Tarantino defamiliarizes the World War II genre movie, creating space to reexamine what we think we know about the era. Ultimately, when *Inglourious Basterds* finally fully embraces the aesthetic of excess Tarantino is famous for in the climactic cinema fire, the moment is constructed in such a way to thwart the viewer's desire to identify with the protagonists and instead positions the viewer as one of the occupying Nazis.

De Groot refers to *Inglourious Basterds* as "historical exploitation" (*Remaking History* 179) and categorizes it as a film that makes "the past something trashy, sensational, excessive, exploitative, flashy—aesthetically part of modernity, rather than a discourse of 'history'" (175). He argues that such an aesthetic brings audience attention to the act of representation and potentially offers audiences a means of seeing through cliché in order to "achieve a better communication of the grimness of events than can be achieved by a discourse—costume drama—that is somehow now a compromised mode" (179). However, the exploitation aesthetic is only one aspect of *Inglourious Basterds*, and it stands in contrast to the way in which Tarantino uses language throughout the film to create an enhanced sense of historical realism. Unlike the majority of mainstream Hollywood films that have an international setting, which typically feature actors speaking English regardless of the characters' purported nationalities, *Inglourious Basterds* has international characters speak in their native languages unless some believable justification for their multilingualism is offered (as when a German and French character opt to converse in English because it is the language both have mastery of). This choice creates a sense of realism that undercuts the expectations of the over-the-top exploitation aesthetic Tarantino has become known for. It also underscores the distance between the viewer and the characters on the screen—a forced reliance on subtitles is a means of hindering straightforward identification and encouraging a more circumspect engagement. This inclusion of and insistence on the foreignness of languages may function as a similar tactic to those examined by Alison Landsberg in *Engaging the Past*; by constantly reminding the audience of the mediated nature of the film's engagement with the past, they create a possible space for the formation of historical consciousness.

The historical consciousness, which Tarantino uses frequently changing aesthetics and languages to foment, is often in direct opposition to the existing understanding of World War II in the historical imaginary. Rather than a clear-cut conflict in which the greatest members of the Greatest Generation triumph over the evils of Nazism on the battlefield, *Inglourious Basterds* focuses on guerrilla warfare, spies, and sabotage. In recruiting the Basterds, Lieutenant Aldo Raine (Brad Pitt) speaks exclusively about the need to do violence to Nazis ("Nazi ain't got no humanity. They're the foot soldiers of a Jew-hatin', mass-murderin' maniac and they need to be destroyed"), without any indication of patriotic sentiment. This is a striking departure from other cinematic monologues that have shaped conceptions of the period. For example, in *Patton* (1970), General George Patton's speech to the troops begins with an affirmation of American triumphalism. Patton declares that "all real Americans love the sting of battle," "Americans play to win all the time," and "Americans have never lost and will never lose a war, because the very thought of losing is hateful to Americans." By contrast, *Inglourious Basterds* does not include any discussion or demonstration of inherent American virtue.

One of Tarantino's most consistent challenges to the historical imaginary throughout the film is this discarding of hagiographic narratives of American participation in World War II. Characters on either side of the conflict are equally likely as individuals to be charming or grating, or to be savvy or incompetent. All engage in acts of extreme brutality toward their enemies, and the film largely relies on the viewer's preexisting knowledge of Nazi crimes to

justify the acts perpetrated against them by the Allied protagonists. Tarantino repeatedly puts the viewer in a position of uncertainty regarding the
motivations of the characters and whether or not to be sympathetic toward
them, thus urging more complex engagements than are present in the historical
imaginary. This can be seen in two of the film's most memorable scenes: the
opening interrogation of a French farmer regarding the whereabouts of his
Jewish neighbors by SS Colonel Hans Landa (Christoph Waltz), and the
behind-enemy-lines infiltration of a tavern populated with Nazi soldiers by
three guerrillas making contact with a spy.

The tavern scene in particular appears to serve primarily as a critique of previous World War II movies that portray such spy work as nearly effortless;
much of the scene's tension arises from the fact that, though he speaks fluent
German, one of the infiltrators (Lieutenant Archie Hicox, played by Michael
Fassbender) raises the suspicion of a gestapo officer with his "very unusual"
(i.e., British) accent. This comes as a surprise to Hicox and the presumed English-
speaking American viewer, who are equally unable to immediately hear the
nuances of German pronunciation. Indeed, Hicox is so confident in his German that he speaks more frequently and loudly than the actual Germans accompanying him, thus drawing the attention of the gestapo in the first place.
Though Hicox is able to offer a convincing story to explain his accent, this
moment of wrong-footedness establishes the extremely tenuous nature of the
deception and creates an environment of heightened tension, in which both
the characters and the viewer increasingly scrutinize every moment for its
potential to raise suspicion. When Hicox finally does blow his cover, leading
to his death and the death of almost everyone else in the tavern, neither he nor
the viewer is meant to know what he did wrong. The moment is not explained
until a later scene, when the tavern's sole survivor tells Raine that Hicox outed
himself by ordering three glasses by holding up three fingers, and the German
gesture for three is two fingers and the thumb. This moment of confusion further underlines the precarity of spy work, in which a literal small gesture can
collapse an entire mission. In an interview with Elvis Mitchell, Tarantino
explains the significance of language to his writing of the film:

> If you can pull off the language, you could survive in enemy territory. . . .
> That's the thing they leave out of other war movies—because in *Where Eagles
> Dare*, German is English and apparently Richard Burton and Clint Eastwood
> speak German so magnificently great all they have to do is put on a costume
> and they can hang out in the general's club. To me—forget about the fact
> I don't buy it, it's also the fact that you've got possibly one of the most
> suspenseful sequences here, but you're pissing it away by English being
> German. ("Brad Pitt & Quentin Tarantino Interview")

While Tarantino's critique of other World War II movies is primarily an artistic one about a wasted storytelling opportunity, he prefaces it with the idea that using English to represent all languages in a multilingual world is insufficiently realistic. In both the opening interrogation and the tavern scene, Tarantino avoids his usual over-the-top aesthetic, minimizing music and editing in favor of focusing viewer attention on the tension between characters and the growing sense of dread that someone will eventually slip up. In terms of their relation to the historical imaginary, these moments establish the film's credibility as a meaningful engagement with the past. Here the history of World War II is presented to the audience in scenes that echo previous cinematic engagements with the era, and the legitimacy of this version is heightened by the use of the complications of language and disguise—something that viewers may not have considered before, but that should immediately ring true—as the primary drivers of suspense and conflict, rather than the so-called excesses that viewers familiar with Tarantino's work have come to expect. Importantly, they also denaturalize the experience of simply watching the movie and instead invite the viewer to apply increased scrutiny to character interactions. This, combined with the use of multiple languages and subtitles and significant consequences for mistakes invisible to both characters and the audience, holds the viewer at a distance from the characters, inviting a more meaningful cognitive engagement with the world of the film.

However, even before the major departure from expected history in the film's third act, *Inglourious Basterds* frequently includes signals (such as title cards, voice-over, and visual and aural homages to 1970s films) to remind the viewer of its fictional nature—oscillating between realism and excess numerous times. The film opens with a title card that reads, "Chapter One: Once upon a Time. . . . . in Nazi-Occupied France," followed by a fade-in on an idyllic hillside farm—a small cottage, laundry hanging on the line, cows, and the figure of a man chopping wood, with an overlaid title giving the year as 1941. The only sound is the diegetic noise of the man's ax hitting the stump at regular intervals until one of his daughters spreads a sheet on the clothesline and, after a moment's hesitation, pulls it back like a curtain to reveal an approaching car and motorcycles. This triggers both the film's soundtrack—an apparent blending of Beethoven's "Für Elise" and music inspired by the well-known themes of Sergio Leone's spaghetti Westerns—and an immediate response from the characters on-screen. The initial moments of quiet realism are thus surrounded by three signals that what we are about to see is fiction, rooting the film primarily in references to performativity and other films rather than in history: the opening of "Once upon a Time. . . . . ," the visual of the sheet acting as a stage curtain, and the beginning of a soundtrack that connects this moment to a specific era and style of genre filmmaking. This aural reference to Leone also raises the possibility of a dual meaning in the chapter title—is it the invocation of a fairy tale, a reference to the Leone film *Once upon a Time in the West*, which shares *Inglourious Basterds'* concern with vengeance as well as stylistic elements, or both?

These choices do, in de Groot's terms, "render explicit the action of representing the past" (*Remaking History* 175), but the fact that the act of representation is alternately foregrounded and diminished throughout the film indicates that this should not be read simply as a film about historical filmmaking. A key element of Tarantino's filmmaking style is pastiche, a combination of recognizable elements from other sources or, in Richard Dyer's definition, "a kind of imitation that you are meant to know is an imitation" (*Pastiche* 1). Dyer argues that pastiche is not necessarily a hollow gesture, but one that can "allow us to feel our connection to the affective frameworks, the structures of feeling, past and present, that we inherit and pass on" (180). While the use of music to evoke a certain mood is an almost universal tool in cinema, Tarantino uses pastiche, particularly aural pastiche, to provide more exact signals to the audience regarding how to feel about the action on-screen. The pastiche of Leone's music to indicate the approaching motorcade is likely a threat, the use of 1970s exploitation film–style title fonts and music to establish Hugo Stiglitz (Til Schweiger) as a single-minded killer of Nazis, and the playing of David Bowie's "Cat People (Putting Out Fire)" as Shosanna prepares for her ultimate plan to burn down her theater on "Nazi Night" all evoke affective connections to previous films or eras of filmmaking and are in keeping with Tarantino's intertextual style.

However, in sequences that are inflected with ambiguity, these signals to the viewer disappear entirely, and their sudden absence creates a greater sense of unease than if Tarantino's pastiche-filled "trash aesthetic" had never been present. To continue the earlier example of the film's beginning: after the arrival of the Nazi motorcade—accompanied by a striking soundtrack, visual cues of the film's fictional nature, and unobtrusive but very active editing (in which the camera cuts between a variety of shots)—SS Colonel Hans Landa (Christoph Waltz) questions the French farmer Monsieur LaPadite alone in the farmhouse. LaPadite's three daughters and the soldiers who accompanied Landa wait outside. Introducing the presence of these characters in order to exclude them heightens the sense of intimacy in the conversation between Landa and LaPadite; they are alone by Landa's design, rather than by chance, leaving the audience to wonder why. At this point the viewer knows very little about the characters. LaPadite is physically imposing, rugged, and taciturn, while Landa appears charming, gregarious, and loquacious. He behaves ingratiatingly as he introduces himself to LaPadite, and his aggressive friendliness as he praises the quality of the milk produced by the farmer's cows and the beauty of his daughters is at odds with the horrors signified by his uniform and rank. The audience thus goes into the scene of their conversation (or interrogation masquerading as conversation) with one character who provides us with very little, and another who purports to provide a great deal but whom we have reason to distrust.

Rather than continuing to signal the audience as to how to feel or what type of story is being told, Tarantino presents this scene with a minimalist aesthetic that stands in stark contrast to the action immediately preceding it. Just as the isolation of Landa and LaPadite is heightened by our having seen the other characters being sent outside, the ambiguous quiet of this scene is heightened by the almost bombastic surplus of meanings provided immediately before. The scene is not accompanied by any music and little editing. Landa and LaPadite sit facing each other, and both are shown in profile. Throughout the scene, the camera is restricted to one of three framings: either a shot in which both men are visible, or a closer view that shows one of the conversation's participants and then the other using shot–reverse shot formation. Throughout, the position of the camera remains unchanged; the men are only shown in profile from the same vantage point. The only exception to this is a brief shot of Shosanna Drey-fus, a young Jewish woman hiding beneath the floorboards with her family, attempting to stifle any noise she may make by covering her mouth. This shot replaces ambiguity with suspense; the viewer now knows that LaPadite is hid-ing the family and Landa is looking for them. The scene's minimalism contin-ues, and neither character indicates the internal state beneath what we now know to be their facade (the farmer's projection of ignorance as to the where-abouts of the Dreyfus family, and the Nazi's projection of genteel friendliness). The scene requires the viewer to attempt to parse the internal states of unread-able characters, without any assistance from the type of visual and aural sig-nals Tarantino has primed viewers to expect through the opening that led in to this moment. The portrayal of the characters here is in contradistinction to the stock types present in the historical imaginary, which does not tend to include charming, solicitous Nazis or gruff, hypermasculine Frenchmen. The narratives of the historical imaginary do not sufficiently prepare a viewer to read the scene, and as a result it asks us to consider what is missing from our understanding of this period. It is not until LaPadite breaks down in tears, betraying the location of the Dreyfus family and watching Landa order their execution, that an aesthetic of excess is reasserted.

By contrast, the climactic scene in which the Nazi high command is destroyed in a burning movie theater, which serves as the Dreyfus family's sole survivor's response to the scene just described, is highly stylized and based far more in a violent demonstration than in dialogue. Shosanna interrupts the film at a moment that is meant to represent the triumph of hegemonic power—the unstoppable soldier calling, "Does anyone have a message for Germany?" She then claims both a voice and visibility, seizing the spotlight and unmasking herself in a near-exact inverse of her introduction huddled beneath the

FIGURE 9 The "giant face" of Shosanna addresses her doomed audience. (Credit: Screenshot from *Inglourious Basterds*.)

floorboards. Rather than a lengthy monologue, in her film she says simply, "I have a message for Germany. That you are all going to die. And I want you to look deep into the face of the Jew that is going to do it. Marcel, burn it down." As the theater rapidly burns due to a fire set by hundreds of nitrate films and those in the cinema scream and attempt to flee, Shosanna's voice can be heard saying, "My name is Shosanna Dreyfus, and this is Jewish vengeance" accompanied by her laughter and her ghostly image reflecting within the ruined cinema.

While Landa could be confident that his position of power meant he could command the attention of whomever he addressed, Shosanna is aware that the Nazis will attempt to reject her words and destroy her person—though the Holocaust is never directly addressed on-screen in *Inglourious Basterds*, it is the near-constant subtext that motivates every Jewish character. It is only through spectacular violence—her "giant face" (as it is referred to in the chapter title that precedes the scene) on-screen and the massive fire consuming the theater—that she can effectively contest the Nazi definition of her. As the "giant face" she destroys the Nazis' attempt to tell their story, puncturing the narrative of hegemonic power with her insistence on her own visibility and self-definition. Her vengeance can also only occur through the mediation of the camera; she forces the Nazis into the position of passive viewers, who have no option to leave or look away, and the fact that she has chosen to make her address through film means that even her death (which occurs before her film plays) cannot silence her. As the theater burns, two of the Basterds burst into the box where Hitler and Goebbels are seated, destroying both beyond all recognition with machine-gun fire.

This is the moment at which the film ruptures, entirely and irrevocably, with the historical imaginary. World War II, at least in Europe, ends in a literal blaze of Jewish fury and vengeance for Nazi crimes. This likely comes as a surprise to the viewer, as it defies the genre conventions of historical fiction. More important, it opens space to consider both the past and the present moment in ways that leaving the historical imaginary unchallenged does not. On the one hand, it is the fulfillment of what is likely a common revenge fantasy—the desire to punish the wrongs of the past as no one who was present at the time did. But it also challenges the conception of the past as something inert and inevitable, asking us to take seriously the possibility that things could very easily have been different than they were.

However, it is also a scene that is very much in discourse with the present moment in its construction. Throughout, Tarantino aligns the viewers with the doomed Nazis and their collaborators rather than with the Jewish characters we have followed up to this point. While the viewer has been positioned to identify with Shosanna throughout the film, it is telling that at this moment in the narrative the spectator has far more in common with the Nazi high command than with the woman seeking to destroy them. The Nazis have gathered in Shosanna's cinema to watch a film that glorifies a World War II victory they are eager to relive. Beyond that, the film they are watching is—judging by the characters' reactions and what little is shown on-screen—a particularly violent one, and one in which the spectators find humor in the violence. While the film has made explicit that all in attendance are Nazis and their French collaborators, they overwhelmingly do not look that way (i.e., many do not wear military uniforms or other symbols of their affiliation). Instead, they appear simply as a large gathering of men and women watching a violent war movie—the exact position of the spectator who in previous moments may have cheered vicious stabbings, beatings, and shootings carried out against their perceived on-screen enemies. Shosanna is interrupting *our* movie as well as theirs—her cut to the Nazi film is also what severs *Inglourious Basterds* from the expectations we have brought to the trajectory of the history we believed it would tell. Most important, Shosanna's on-screen persona hails the cinema audience in English, despite the fact that her supposed audience is German-speaking, and that *Inglourious Basterds* has already established that the character speaks only French. In spite of saying that her message is for Germany, it is the contemporary American audience that has been forced into the position of the startled Nazis. Tarantino's construction of a shared moment of spectatorship between contemporary viewers of his film and Nazi viewers of the film within it suggests a shared complicity between the two groups. This moment encourages us to consider our culpability in the present moment—who is being victimized by state violence, and where do we stand in the conflict?

Inglourious Basterds was positively reviewed for its artistic merits, but its portrayal of Jewish characters engaged in violent revenge against the Nazis was controversial. As discussed by Rosenfeld in *Hi, Hitler!*, some critics celebrated the way the film "liberated the Jew from his cinematic role as victim" (285), while others "objected to the film's fictional depiction of Jews doing to the Nazis what they had actually suffered at their hands in real history" (286). This concern is likely rooted in Tarantino's decision to rely almost entirely on the viewer's knowledge of the Holocaust as sufficient motivation for its Jewish characters. While the Basterds and Shosanna do enact brutal violence against the Nazis, it is entirely focused on military targets. To say the film portrays Jews as acting like Nazis because they engage in brutality against Nazi soldiers is to lose sight of the systematic murder of millions of civilians that defines the Nazi regime (even in Tarantino's film, it is only Nazis who are shown killing civilians). According to Rosenfeld, the film was also seen by various critics as both supportive and critical of Israeli state actions toward the Palestinian people; it was alternately read as an affirmation of the need for strong military self-defense for Israel and an unflattering depiction of Jews as terrorists (287). This wide variety of critical readings demonstrates the challenges of legibility outside the bounds of the historical imaginary but also demonstrates some of the ways in which challenging accepted narratives can open spaces for new kinds of understanding of both the past and how it reflects on the present. *Inglourious Basterds* is undoubtedly a messy engagement with cinematic depictions and popular understandings of World War II in Europe, but that messiness is potentially useful in disrupting the overly tidy narratives that have come to dominate the historical imaginary.

Django Unchained

Tarantino followed *Inglourious Basterds* with another film likely to fit the categorization of historical exploitation, *Django Unchained* (2012). Like *Inglourious Basterds*, *Django Unchained* addresses a systemic historical atrocity through the lens of a revenge fantasy; while *Inglourious Basterds* depicted American and French Jews seeking spectacular revenge on the Nazi high command and their collaborators for the horrors of the Holocaust, *Django Unchained* is the story of a freed slave's destruction of the beneficiaries of the plantation system and those who support them as vengeance for the degradations he and his wife have suffered. *Django Unchained* follows Django, a slave who is bought, freed, and befriended by King Schultz, a white bounty hunter who needs his help finding the men who were once overseers at the plantation where he lived. After those men are dispatched, Schultz convinces Django to become his business partner for the winter, with the understanding that in the spring they will return to Mississippi to find and free Django's wife, Hildy (which, to Schultz's surprise, is short for the German name Broomhilda). They find she has been purchased by Calvin Candie, a wealthy plantation owner whose main hobby is forcing slaves to fight to the death for his amusement. They feign the intention of purchasing one of his fighters for a high price in order to gain access to the plantation and find Hildy. Throughout *Django Unchained*, Tarantino seeks to mediate two narratives of American slavery that compete for primacy in the American historical imaginary, using alternately aestheticized and gruesome violence to contest portrayals of slavery that romanticize the antebellum South or portray chattel slavery as unfortunate but palatable. *Django Unchained* ultimately rejects the depiction of slavery as the result of a few bad actors or simply a product of its time. Instead it seeks to implicate all who benefited from or tolerated slavery, as well as contemporary viewers in the perpetuation of racial violence.

Though *Django Unchained*, like *Inglourious Basterds*, was well reviewed (the two films earned 88 percent and 89 percent, respectively, on the review aggregate site *Rotten Tomatoes*), it proved to be a more controversial film. In all likelihood, this is because American chattel slavery remains a more controversial topic in the United States than the Holocaust—whether slavery was really "all that bad," continues to be the subject of mainstream debates about history in a way the events of the Holocaust are not. For example, a 2014 review (later withdrawn) of Edward Baptist's *The Half Has Never Been Told: Slavery and the Making of American Capitalism* in the *Economist* included the following critique: "Mr. Baptist has not written an objective history of slavery. Almost all the blacks in his book are victims, almost all the whites villains. This is not history; it is advocacy." In response to criticism, the *Economist* issued an apology in which it acknowledged, "Slavery was an evil system, in which the great majority of victims were blacks, and the great majority of whites involved in slavery were willing participants and beneficiaries of that evil" ("Our Withdrawn Review"). It remains striking, however, that this clarification was necessary, and that a review which assumed a true work of "history" would find the ways in which the system of slavery did not uniquely oppress Black people or reflect poorly on white people in the name of objectivity was published at all. In another revealing instance, during her speech at the 2016 Democratic National Convention, Michelle Obama mentioned the fact that the White House had been built by slaves (a well-documented historical reality). As described in the *New York Times*, this fact "was met with derision and disbelief by some, who questioned whether it was true and said her choice to mention it amounted to an attempt to divide the country along racial lines" (Davis). These instances illustrate how the realities of slavery and its atrocities remain up for debate in mainstream discourse, unlike the accepted history of Nazi atrocities in World War II.

In terms of the historical imaginary, the history of slavery remains more in flux in the United States than many other aspects of the nation's past—idyllic images of the antebellum South from magnolia myth films like *Gone with the Wind* (1939) compete with those, like the landmark miniseries *Roots* (1977), that attempt to unflinchingly portray the horrors of slavery. Understandings of the historical imaginary have come to uneasy compromises in their narratives of slavery as bad, but not unpalatably so. Individuals who owned slaves, particularly Founding Fathers, may still be beloved and admired, and are defended today as products of their time who did not and could not be expected to know better. This sanitized version of slavery's history is often challenged but has not yet been overthrown. As a result of this continuing tension, any major Hollywood film about slavery faces intense scrutiny from an array of viewers with strongly held stakes in the depiction of that chapter in American history—those seeking a depiction of slavery that is not so negative as to be troubling, or at least one that provides sympathetic white characters with which to identify, and those seeking a depiction that challenges the sanitized view of American history and provides a "realistic" depiction of a system of oppression that has been given sparse on-screen attention over the years.

Django Unchained seems almost intentionally crafted to trouble both groups. The film goes out of its way to show, in often-grotesque imagery, the violent degradations of slavery, which serve as a constant challenge to the persistent myths of benevolent slave ownership. In addition to scenes that show slaves being whipped, which have come to be expected in depictions of slavery, *Django Unchained* depicts tortures that most viewers are unlikely to have seen before, involving pronged iron collars, iron gags, and a hot box. Django is nearly castrated at one point, and his wife, Hildy, is offered as a sexual plaything to multiple men. In a particularly gruesome scene, a slave who has attempted to escape is ripped apart by dogs. Later, there are unexpected flashbacks to this scene, so even those viewers who choose to avert their eyes when the moment initially occurs will be forced to see images from it. The plot is driven, in part, by the practice of "Mandingo fighting," forcing slaves to fight to the death for their owners' amusement, and one such fight is shown at length. In all these choices, *Django Unchained* seeks to intentionally challenge narratives that portray slavery as "not so bad" or are more interested in the perceived glamour of the antebellum plantation than in examining the suffering on which it was built.

However, *Django Unchained* provides a white benefactor and mentor for Django in the character of Dr. King Schultz, who frees Django from slavery, offers him a path forward as his partner in bounty hunting, teaches him to read and shoot, masterminds their plan to free Django's wife from her enslavement, and ultimately kills the sadistic plantation owner, Calvin Candie (portrayed by Leonardo DiCaprio). In his critique of the film, actor and activist Jesse

Williams argues that it is Schultz, rather than Django, who is the film's true hero, and that Black characters exhibit little agency or interest in obtaining their freedom. Williams also argues that while Tarantino has stated the film's near-constant use of "n—-" in dialogue is in the service of "authenticity," that commitment to authenticity disappears when actually depicting historical conditions. Williams notes that the film almost completely ignores the existence of slaves forced to work in the fields, much less their backbreaking labor. In describing Candie's plantation, Williams writes, "Is this one of those rare slave plantations that primarily trades in polished silverware and gossip? That authenticity card that Tarantino used to buy all those 'n—-s' has an awfully selective memory." This and other inaccuracies about the material reality of plantation life lead Williams to describe *Django Unchained* as a "lazy, oversimplified reduction of our history."

As in *Inglourious Basterds*, Tarantino seems to be seeking a visceral response, one that raises questions about the past via imaginative engagement rather than a conveyance of historical fact. This is a potentially useful means of challenging the historical imaginary; by pushing the viewer toward a different kind of affective engagement with the past, Tarantino may trigger a reexamination of what has previously been uncritically accepted. In an interview with Terry Gross, Tarantino states: "There haven't been that many slave narratives in the last 40 years of cinema, and usually when there are, they're usually done on television, and for the most part . . . they're historical movies, like history with a capital H. . . . And that can be fine, well enough, but for the most part they keep you at arm's length dramatically. Because also there is this kind of level of good taste that they're trying to deal with . . . and frankly oftentimes they just feel like dusty textbooks just barely dramatized" ("Quentin Tarantino, 'Unchained' and Unruly"). Like *Inglourious Basterds, Django Unchained* does not attempt to function as a text that teaches a given history but as one in which the audience is encouraged to imagine a particular history in an unexpected way. This challenges the sense of inevitability that often accompanies the telling of historical events and encourages viewers to consider themselves as active in their own historic moment. While most of the dramatic devices Tarantino draws on have some basis in history, the "Mandingo fighting," notably, does not. Rather, this device originated in the 1975 blaxploitation film *Mandingo*—a genre of which Tarantino is a well-known enthusiast (Harris). Both this, and the quote provided earlier, indicate that *Django Unchained* is, in many ways, a direct response to understandings of the history of slavery that are firmly ensconced in the historical imaginary but were not generated by conventional historical methods.

As Linda Williams argues in *Playing the Race Card*, the history of slavery in the United States and, by extension, contemporary race relations have been worked and reworked through media since before the Civil War. She identifies two conflicting narratives of American racial identity—"the vision of a black man beaten by a white and the responding 'counter' vision of the white woman endangered or raped by the emancipated and uppity black villain" (5). Williams sees the former as originating in the Harriet Beecher Stowe novel *Uncle Tom's Cabin* (and particularly its stage and early screen adaptations) and the latter as first crystallizing in D. W. Griffith's notorious film *The Birth of a Nation* (1915). Williams writes that these two narratives are foundational texts in the formation of American identity, and their uses of melodrama—either in "discovering the suffering humanity of slaves" or in introducing "the racially threatened white woman" (7)—continue to be the narratives by which we understand the history and contemporary reality of race in the United States. In spite of their conflicting nature, both of these narratives are present in the historical imaginary.

Django Unchained's intervention into the historical imaginary is that it attempts to rework both of these narratives simultaneously; the film draws on the familiar tropes established in melodramas of suffering Black bodies outlined by Williams, but it also works to subvert what she refers to as the "'anti-Tom' reversal" (7) generated in works such *The Birth of a Nation*. The suffering inflicted on Django and other slaves throughout the film is of a piece with previous narratives' "generation of 'moral legibility' (Brooks, 1995, cited in Williams, 2001) through the spectacle of racialized bodily suffering" (xiv). However, Django's response to his suffering is a marked departure from that of the Black protagonists of other melodramatic works. In *Uncle Tom's Cabin*, as well as in *Roots*, the Black men through whose bodily suffering the audience sees the outrage of slavery and the indefensibility of the slave system ultimately die at the end of their torment. Tom is beaten to death after refusing to betray the location of two escaped slaves, and Kunta Kinte, the founding patriarch of the family whose story *Roots* follows, endures whipping and the severing of his foot, as well as the emotional trauma of family separation when his wife and daughter are sold to different plantations before he dies. Django, by contrast, does not perform perfect victimhood in response to his suffering. After entering into partnership with Schultz, Django ultimately kills all the white people (with the exception of Calvin Candie, who is dispatched by Schultz) who have worked to support the plantations where he and his wife endured the traumas of slavery: the overseers who beat them; the slave catchers who apprehend Hildy and other slaves in their attempts to escape; the henchmen who threaten and torture Django; Calvin Candie's sister, who supervises the prostituting of attractive slaves like Hildy to plantation guests; and the head house slave, whose near-minstrel levels of obsequious devotion to Candie mask the fact that he masterminds much of the plantation's management.

While Django's vengeance is thematically of a piece with the Jewish vengeance portrayed in *Inglourious Basterds*, it is a dramatic departure from the responses to racial violence that have been deemed acceptable in discourses around slavery and its aftermath. In the United States, the victims of slavery are seen as a threat to the current social order in a way the victims of the Holocaust are not; as a result, claims that Black men are innocent victims of racial violence continue to be aggressively interrogated in media discourses. The framing of Black men as inherently criminal and threatening has persisted for centuries, and must be addressed before Black men can be conceived of as victims. One real-world example of someone who successfully navigated those narratives is Mamie Till, the mother of lynching victim Emmett Till, who mobilized her son's murder as a major moment in civil rights history. In an interview with Rich Juzwiak, Timothy Tyson, author of *The Blood of Emmett Till*, argues that Mamie Till "dramatizes the lynching of her son as a way to topple the social order that killed him," and she was able to do so, in part, because she was savvy enough to rescript part of the events that led to his killing. As Tyson recounts:

> She knows that any perception of sexual interest or sexual playfulness from her son to Carolyn Bryant will turn that into justifiable homicide in the unconsciousness of America, but also in the literal sense, and so regarding the whistling piece of it, she says, "He had a speech impediment and so I told him if he couldn't get his words out to whistle." That's just a fabrication, but she's spinning a difficult piece of it—he did whistle at [Bryant], that's sort of agreed upon—but she's trying to get America to look at his humanity and to look at the inhumanity of the racial caste system in America.

Tyson's description of Mamie Till's recognition of the need to shift the narrative of her son's lynching from, in Williams's terms, an "anti-Tom" to a "Tom" narrative in order to establish her son's killing as unjust continues to be relevant in the contemporary media landscape, where victims of racial violence such as Michael Brown, Trayvon Martin, and Eric Garner are argued to have somehow brought on their deaths by alleged wrongdoings in their lives prior to their final moments. Throughout American history to the present moment, Black men's claims to victimhood have been routinely rejected because of the presumption that Black men cannot be innocent.

While racial melodramas such as *Uncle Tom's Cabin* tend to combat this presumption by portraying the suffering Black man as beyond reproach, *Django Unchained* instead rejects the impulse to shape its hero as a martyr in order to claim audience sympathy. Like his cinematic predecessors, Django suffers the physical traumas and humiliations of slavery. However, rather than remaining morally superior by remaining unbroken in spirit and refusing to sink to his oppressors' level of cruelty, thus creating the easy moral legibility typical of melodrama, Django eagerly repays humiliation with humiliation. When he encounters the overseers who whipped his wife, he first shoots the one who mocked his pleas to spare her, repeating back the overseer's sadistic "I like the way you beg, boy," as "I like the way you die, boy." He then drops his gun and takes up the whip himself, brutally beating the second overseer as he squirms on the ground. When Django realizes other slaves are watching him, his rage at seeing the men he could not prevent from torturing his wife fades, and he calmly asks, "Y'all want to see something?" before once again taking up his gun and shooting the beaten man multiple times.

This moment is the first illustration of a theme that continues for the length of the movie, wherein in order to free his wife and seek revenge for what they have suffered, Django repeatedly duplicates the actions or attitudes of his hated oppressors. To infiltrate Candie's plantation, Django takes on the role of a Black slaver, which forces him to berate slaves and overrule Schultz's attempt to save the enslaved d'Artagnan from being eaten by dogs. Their charade ultimately fails, but in the final scene Django once again echoes the actions of his oppressors with his own in enacting his revenge. Like the movie theater finale of *Inglourious Basterds*, the conclusion of *Django Unchained* is a dramatic departure from expected history, in which the forces of hegemonic power are abruptly overturned rather than preserved in the name of historical authenticity.

Django's mirroring of his despicable tormentors throughout the film does not, in turn, reduce him to a despicable figure, but it does render him more morally complex than the typical protagonist of a racial melodrama. One way in which the film elevates Django above his antagonists is through its portrayal of their violence. The violence enacted by the proponents of the slave system is graphic and difficult to watch—Hildy being whipped, d'Artagnan being devoured by dogs, and Django nearly being castrated are all moments that repel the viewer with visceral gruesomeness. Django's violence, by contrast, is highly aestheticized—the camera lingers admiringly on Django in outlandish costumes striking powerful poses, and one of the film's most famous shots is a highly aestheticized, lingering image of the vibrant red blood of an executed overseer sprayed across bright white cotton. The violence inflicted by Django is shot to be attractive rather than gruesome and is condoned by Tarantino's aesthetic of excess.

In the film's finale, Django appears at the top of the house's staircase, wearing Candie's clothes and smoking with his cigarette holder, a visual display of his contempt for a man and system that positioned Django as lower. Rather than an inherent inferior, as Candie insists Django is via a monologue about phrenology, Django is positioning himself as in every way equal to and above the beneficiaries of plantation life. In Homi Bhabha's terms, Django is offering resistance through mimicry, a moment in which "the look of surveillance returns as the displacing gaze of the disciplined, where the observer becomes the observed and 'partial' representation rearticulates the whole notion of *identity*" (129; emphasis in original). Django uses his gun to castrate Billy Crash,

Candie's henchman who gleefully attempted to do the same to him earlier in the film, and kills Candie's sister after first instructing an enslaved woman to say goodbye to her—a nod to the insidious gentility with which the woman has participated in the functioning of the plantation. Django then instructs the remaining slaves to flee, except Stephen, the head house slave.

Throughout the film, Stephen (Samuel L. Jackson) is revealed to be the true mastermind behind the plantation on which he lives. While he performs over-the-top subservience around other people, in private with Calvin Candie he shows himself to be the equal, or even superior, of his supposed master. He is also the one who recognizes the connection between Hildy and Django, ruining Django's attempt to buy his wife's freedom, and it is Stephen who devises Django's punishment for his role in the death of Calvin Candie. While on the surface it may seem unsatisfying that it is Schultz, not Django, who kills Calvin Candie, the fact that the film continues well after Candie's death indicates that he is not the true villain, despite what the audience has been led to expect. The plantation continues to exist, and the system by which it is run will remain unchanged, without him. While Candie is the primary beneficiary of the plantation system, he does not have the power to perpetuate it alone. By setting Django against Candie's supporters and collaborators in the final scene, this film, much like *Inglourious Basterds* is making a larger argument about systemic oppression—that it is the collaborators who capitulate to hegemonic power for their own benefit (however minimal) who bear the greatest responsibility for its perpetuation. This plays out in Django's final confrontation with Stephen, as Django asserts his superiority to the plantation system. As he descends the staircase toward Stephen he says, "Seventy-six years, Stephen. How many n——s you think you seen come and go? Seven thousand? Eight thousand? Nine thousand? Nine thousand nine hundred and ninety nine? Every single word that came out of Calvin Candie's mouth was nothing but horseshit, but he was right about one thing: I am that one n——in ten thousand." As Django speaks, he descends the stairs toward Stephen, and the low angle emphasizes him as a powerful figure. The light shining from above causes the outline of his hat to take on the appearance of a halo, lending him the appearance of almost supernatural power. Stephen largely ignores what Django says, instead screaming and cursing at him, vowing that the plantation can never be destroyed. Django, in turn, ignores Stephen, setting off a fuse and completing his destruction of the authority built on Candie's words by having both the plantation house and Stephen consumed in a massive fireball.

The main way in which *Django Unchained* counters the melodramatic impulse to make Django sympathetic through a performance of perfect, noble, suffering is by inverting the typical "anti-Tom," melodramatic narrative. Rather than focusing on a sexually threatened white woman, *Django Unchained* is instead driven by the danger faced by a sexually threatened Black woman. The only reason the film seems to include a white woman at all, in the form of Calvin Candie's sister, Lara Lee Candie-Fitzwilly, is so that the protagonists can ignore her. The only man who shows any interest in her at all is her own brother, whose somewhat too-intense fixation on his sister belies a troubling dynamic between the two and on the historic territoriality of white men around the sexuality of white women. Hildy, by contrast, spends the entire film facing the threat of rape and forced prostitution—first simply because she is a beautiful, enslaved woman, and then as retribution for her husband's actions. It is thus Hildy's virtue, rather than Django's, that must remain beyond reproach for the morality of the film to function (in melodramatic terms, at least), and Hildy who performs noble, uncomplaining suffering. An unfortunate side effect of this is that Hildy is dramatically underwritten and functions more as a MacGuffin motivating her husband than an individual with agency and ambitions of her own.

Django Unchained works to disrupt both the cinematic history and contemporary discourses of race in the American historical imaginary by subverting the two melodramatic discourses that have structured our understanding of the topic. In its final scene, *Django Unchained* defies audience expectations of how a story about slavery must end—with the system of slavery either intact or ended with the conclusion of the Civil War. While the broader slave system continues to exist as Django and Hildy ride off from the smoldering ashes of Candie Land, this particular plantation (contrary to Stephen's final words) is gone forever. Django's successful vengeance and his focus on Candie's enablers, rather than on Candie himself, invite the viewer to consider the fact that the trajectory of the history of slavery was not inevitable, and it was sustained for hundreds of years not by a few villainous individuals but by widespread collaborative effort and indifference to Black suffering. The film consistently challenges the narratives of the historical imaginary in which slavery is simply an unfortunate chapter of American history by insisting on its horrific practices and foregrounding its protagonist's righteous rage, rather than a more palatable performance of victimhood.

Once upon a Time . . . in Hollywood

Tarantino's most recent alternate history film is *Once upon a Time . . . in Hollywood* (2019), which follows fictional protagonists Rick Dalton (Leonardo DiCaprio), a fading star trying to revive his career, and Cliff Booth (Brad Pitt), his stunt man/driver, as they drift through and around Los Angeles in 1969. Peripheral but ever present is Sharon Tate (Margot Robbie), Dalton's next-door neighbor and the most famous victim of the Tate-LaBianca murders committed by followers of Charles Manson in August 1969. The young women of the

Manson family also wander along the periphery of the movie, intersecting with the main story line once when Booth gives the fictional Manson family member Pussycat a ride to Spahn Ranch only to come into conflict with Manson's followers due to his investigation of George Spahn's well-being, and again the night of August 8, 1969. The film's often languid, dreamy pacing is in constant tension with both the audience's knowledge that the characters are unknowingly approaching the gruesome murders widely described as ending the 1960s and the expectation, rooted in the notorious counterfactuality of *Inglourious Basterds* (of which *Once upon a Time . . . in Hollywood* offers an early, winking pastiche) and *Django Unchained*, that Tarantino will depart from known history and the audience will see a version of the past in which Tate's life is spared. Ultimately, the film both fulfills and thwarts viewer expectations, providing a meditation on liminality and exploring the sometimes illusory and sometimes impassible nature of temporal and spatial boundaries.

Like *Inglourious Basterds* and *Django Unchained*, *Once upon a Time . . . in Hollywood* was well reviewed. However, the film came under scrutiny for its depiction of two nonfictional characters—Sharon Tate and Bruce Lee. Initially the film was scheduled to be released on the fiftieth anniversary of Tate's murder, an exploitative publicity choice that Tate's surviving sister, Debra, objected to. Tarantino arranged to meet with Debra Tate to discuss her concerns about the film, allowed her to review the script, discussed her sister with her, and invited her to the set on the day Margot Robbie shot Sharon Tate's most consequential scene in the film. This, along with Sony's decision to change the release date, allayed Debra Tate's concerns, and she became an advocate for the film. Tate assured viewers before it came out, "This movie is not what people would expect it to be when you combine the Tarantino and Manson names" (Marotta). After the film's release, she told *Vanity Fair* that Robbie's performance was so effective that "she made me cry because she sounded just like Sharon. [. . .] The front of my shirt was wet. I actually got to see my sister again nearly fifty years later" (Miller).

Debra Tate was not the only source of critique of Tarantino's depiction of her sister. At the film's Cannes premiere, *New York Times* reporter Farah Nayeri asked Tarantino why Sharon Tate had so few lines of dialogue in the film, to which the director responded tersely, "Well, I just reject your hypothesis" (Nayeri). Other outlets picked up on the tense exchange, and there was some critical discussion of the perceived choice to silence or sideline Tate in favor of the fictional male protagonists, despite Tate's real-life tragic death being the apparent impetus for the story. However, the film's decision to keep Tate at a distance from the viewer is necessary for the particular relation to history the film is exploring—one of longing and missed opportunity. As described in *Vulture*, the Sharon Tate of *Once upon a Time . . . in Hollywood* "is a character who is often looked at and talked about but who rarely has a voice. This also aligns with the shape her career had taken at the time: While she had a lot of talent, she was often cast for her beauty, and was often known more for her photo shoots than her performances" (Ebiri). More important, this depiction aligns with how she has been remembered since her murder—beautiful, but inaccessible and silent, remembered primarily for the gruesome tragedy that ended her life, and referenced almost exclusively in connection with Manson and her husband, Roman Polanski.

Once upon a Time . . . in Hollywood often looks longingly and poignantly at Tate (almost every review mentions the affecting scene where Robbie-as-Tate goes to a movie theater and watches the actual Sharon Tate's performance in *The Wrecking Crew* [1968]), but the film refuses to grant the viewer the closeness or insight to her interiority that conventions of period film have led them to expect. Sharon Tate remains an ephemeral figure of fantasy throughout the film—more fairy princess in her distant tower than up-and-coming Hollywood actress—because she has come to represent an inaccessible lost innocence; her death was the death of Hollywood's fantasy of itself, and this is a film about the fantasy that remains at a respectful distance from the individual.

Unfortunately, the same cannot be said of the film's depiction of Bruce Lee, which is gratuitously inaccurate, disrespectful, and without purpose. Aside from being shown briefly in flashback training Sharon Tate in martial arts for *The Wrecking Crew* (a historically accurate detail), Lee is prominently featured in an extended sequence, a flashback ostensibly illustrating why Cliff Booth is no longer able to get work as a stuntman. The scene shows Lee engaged in a self-aggrandizing monologue about boxing and martial arts to crew members of the series *The Green Hornet* (1966–1967) between takes. When Booth scoffs at Lee's assertion that he would win in a fight against Cassius Clay (Muhammad Ali), Lee immediately takes offense and demands to know what Booth thinks is funny. Booth, smirking and self-possessed, attempts to defuse the moment, saying, "I don't want any trouble, I'm just here to do a job." Lee persists in the exchange until Booth tells him, "You're a little man with a big mouth and a big chip." Lee, still posturing for his audience of crew members and bit players, tells Booth that he would like to fight him, but, he says, "my hands are registered as lethal weapons. That means we get into a fight, I accidentally kill you, I go to jail." Booth mockingly counters that anyone who accidentally kills someone in a fight goes to jail for manslaughter, and the two agree to a two-out-of-three-round fight, which ultimately ends in a tie when they are interrupted before the third round.

Like Sharon Tate, Bruce Lee died tragically young; he was thirty-two when he passed away, likely from complications caused by heat stroke. And like Tate, Lee has surviving relatives who care deeply for him as an individual and for the public persona he represents in media. However, Tarantino showed Lee's legacy and family none of the consideration that Tate's received. Lee's daughter,

Shannon Lee, had no insight into how her father would be portrayed in the movie before its premiere. After seeing the film, she said, "It was really uncomfortable to sit in the theater and listen to people laugh at my father," claiming that Tarantino had treated him "the way that white Hollywood did when he was alive." She criticized the film for its depiction of her father as "an arrogant asshole who was full of hot air," a point echoed by Bruce Lee biographer Matthew Polly, who called attention to the difference between the film's respectful portrayals of Sharon Tate, Jay Sebring, and Steve McQueen versus its use of Bruce Lee, "the only non-white character in the film. [Tarantino] could have achieved the same effect—using Bruce to make Brad Pitt's character look tough—without the mockery" (Molloy). Shannon Lee made clear that her issue was not with Tarantino's inclusion of her father in the film, or even his use of Bruce Lee as a means to make Cliff Booth look tough—"I understand they want to make the Brad Pitt character this super bad-ass who could beat up Bruce Lee"—but the stereotyping portrayal that ignored "who Bruce Lee was as a human being and how he lived his life. All of that was flushed down the toilet in this portrayal, and [the film] made my father into this arrogant punching bag."

Tarantino shrugged off all critique of his portrayal of Bruce Lee, responding to questions about such criticisms at the film's Moscow press conference by saying, "Bruce Lee was kind of an arrogant guy . . . if people are saying, 'Well he never said he could beat up Mohammad Ali,' well yeah he did. Alright?" He also dismissed fans' unhappiness with the outcome of the fight between Bruce Lee and Cliff Booth, saying, "If you ask me the question, 'Who would win in a fight: Bruce Lee or Dracula?' It's the same question. It's a fictional character. If I say Cliff can beat Bruce Lee up, he's a fictional character so he could beat Bruce Lee up" (Sharf). The dismissal attempts to foreclose discussion of both accuracy and imagination—it claims both that the film represents Bruce Lee accurately and that the film is immune to criticism because it depicts a fictional encounter. Shannon Lee pointed out that the passage from a book by Linda Lee Caldwell (Bruce Lee's widow) that posited Bruce Lee would win in a fight against Muhammad Ali did not come from Bruce Lee or Linda Lee but from an admirer of Lee's work. Indeed, in his 1987 book, *The Making of Enter the Dragon*, that film's director quoted Bruce Lee as saying, "Everybody says I must fight Ali some day. I'm studying every move he makes. I'm getting to know how he thinks and moves. . . . Look at my hand. That's a little Chinese hand. He'd kill me" (Norris). But there is no indication that any amount of documentation could cause Tarantino to reconsider the accuracy or the ethics of his portrayal of Lee. The scene is a jarring moment of hostility toward the film's only featured character of color, emphasizing how absolutely Tarantino envisions 1960s Hollywood as an exclusively white space.

The flashback that includes the five inexcusable minutes spent denigrating Bruce Lee is framed by one of the film's many moments of using sound to indicate permeability of presumed boundaries. Cliff Booth arrives at Rick Dalton's house to repair the television antenna on the roof. As the car winds up the hill toward Dalton's home in the Hollywood Hills, the camera tracks its approach—above and from a distance. Booth is not visible inside the car, but the car radio is clearly audible as he approaches and pulls into the driveway. Aerial shots of vehicles accompanied by the sound of the car's radio (but none of the other sounds or potential conversations inside the vehicle) are a repeated motif of the film. While many scenes are shot in cars' interiors, there are also numerous moments in which the viewer is denied that access. Throughout the film, cars are treated as bounded spaces that the viewer is not automatically enti-tled to see within—car doors may close with the same finality as doors to a home we are not invited within. But that visual boundary cannot contain the aural. Sound escapes, providing our only clues to what is going on within.

To reach the roof of Dalton's house, Booth uses his stunt man physical acu-men to jump first on top of a gate, then onto the top of the brick wall separat-ing Dalton's home from the Polanksi-Tate residence next door, then to the roof. As he reaches the antenna and prepares to begin work, the camera slowly pans left and pulls back, revealing first thick, bushy trees on the Polanski-Tate side of the wall (a second visually obscuring barrier to reinforce the wall) and finally the second story of the house, just visible beyond the branches. Dalton seems not to notice the Polanski-Tate house, until he hears music coming from it, at which point he turns away from the camera and tilts his head, apparently try-ing to look past the trees to parse the source of a Paul Revere and the Raiders record album.

The scene then cuts to a shot of a record player inside the Polanski-Tate home, and Sharon Tate is shown starting the record. She smiles to herself, closes her eyes, and dances. This is how Tate is often seen throughout the film—dancing, smiling at some inner joke, or joyfully greeting her friends. In a film cen-tered on characters, most notably Rick Dalton, who are preoccupied with temporality—reflecting on opportunities acquired or missed, mistakes made or avoided, a future that may be humiliating or glorious—Sharon Tate is always fully in the moment. Tate dances out of frame, and for a moment she is visible only as an obscured reflection in the window, bobbing happily to the music as she folds clothes and places them into a suitcase. Even with the camera osten-sibly within the intimate space of Sharon Tate's bedroom, the viewer's access to her is limited. She is an enticing but inaccessible echo.

Tate's music appears to be the impetus that triggers Booth's reflective flash-back to his confrontation with Bruce Lee—the choice that led to his being essentially unemployable as a television stuntman and resulted in his now spending the day attending to Rick Dalton's antenna. This directly links Sharon Tate with the concept of memory in the film. It is the presence of Tate that pulls Booth into considering his own past, but their connection remains entirely in liminal space—they are separated by a wall, foliage, and a home. As the flashback ends, Booth can still hear Paul Revere and the Raiders from Tate's record player, though the song has changed. However, the scene does not end here, despite Booth having reached the conclusion of both his ruminations and his repair work. As it continues, the scene further explores the affective potential of Sharon Tate's connection with liminality, now attempting to trigger memory and agitation in the audience instead of in another character.

Booth remains on the roof (smoking and listening to Tate's music) after his work on the antenna is complete. He now occupies the observational position from which the camera watched his own drive to Dalton's house. From there, he sees a van pull up and park along the curb outside the Polanski-Tate residence. He watches the van, which is in poor repair and out of place in the wealthy neighborhood, with clear suspicion. He then scrutinizes the distant figure of a thin man with shoulder length brown hair who gets out and approaches the Polanski-Tate home. The average viewer will quickly deduce that this is Charles Manson. Though Booth does not react to Manson's arrival, he appears to sense something amiss. However, from Booth's perspective on the roof, Manson's mood and intent are entirely inscrutable.

The scene cuts to the interior, where Sharon is still packing. The song "Hunger" by Paul Revere and the Raiders fills the house. The lyrics, including "I'm hungry for that sweet life" and "There's a custom-tailored world that I wanna own someday" are evocative of Manson's desires for fame and recognition, the thwarting of which led him to order his followers to their infamous crimes. Tate laughs and teases Jay Sebring for dancing to the uncool album with her. The close connection between the former-lovers-now-friends was explained to an acquaintance by Steve McQueen (who, in reality, delivered the eulogy at Sebring's funeral after his murder by Manson's followers) in a previous scene. The light tone in the house contrasts with the impending approach by Manson, which the viewer is aware of but Tate and Sebring are not. At this point that approach is both literal (as we, with Booth, have seen Manson's walk toward the house) and figurative—as the audience's dread of the Tate-LaBianca murders is brought into queasy focus. A blurry and distant Manson comes into view through the window over Tate's shoulder (their reflections even briefly overlap), and the scene becomes one of horror movie–style dramatic irony. The audience knows the monster's arrival is imminent, but Tate and Sebring remain oblivious.

Sebring spots Manson out the window and goes outside to find out what this "shaggy asshole" is doing in his friend's driveway. Shortly after, Tate follows, standing in the doorway and asking who it is. The interaction between the three is banal—Manson introduces himself as a friend of the house's former occupants and asks if Sebring knows where they have moved to. Sebring says he does not and sends Manson on his way, and Manson departs with a polite "Ma'am" and a wave to Tate. Tate and Sebring appear to find Manson unsettling but not threatening. When Tate appears in the doorway and asks, "Who is it, Jay?" he responds, "It's OK, honey," and she gives a slight smile and perfunctory wave to Manson as he departs.

The effectiveness of this scene relies on the audience's engagement with the tension between knowledge of the real-life tragedy that ended the lives of Tate and Sebring and the hope, rooted in Tarantino's now established tendency to depart from known history, that this time they may avert that outcome. This engagement is one of contingency, what Barbie Zelizer defines as "the quality of being uncertain, conditional, or (im)possible" (6). Zelizer's interest in contingency is rooted in journalistic practices around images of people taken moments before their death, and the varied forms of response they may illicit. However, the portrayal of Tate in *Once upon a Time . . . in Hollywood* functions as an extended "about to die" image. Like the images of contingency analyzed by Zelizer, scenes such as this one with Tate "introduce chance, relativity, implication, and hypothesis into the act of viewing. . . . The imagination offers the possibility to interpret in a fanciful, illogical, baseless, or irrational fashion" (6). The audience's desire to see Sharon Tate escape her murderers fifty years after her death is just such a fanciful or irrational engagement with contingency.

Encounters with contingency, which are depicted in *Once upon a Time . . . in Hollywood* as occurring at liminal moments, can trigger a variety of responses. Like the departures from the historical record of *Inglourious Basterds* and *Django Unchained*, liminality in *Once upon a Time . . . in Hollywood* makes an argument for the past as a space of possibility—one where alternative understandings remain available, where other paths could have been taken, and where imagination enables meaningful knowledge. The key difference is that, unlike the protagonists of *Inglourious Basterds* and *Django Unchained*, Sharon Tate does not represent alternate responses to systemic atrocities, but an individual crime. The film centers her as an individual—vibrant, beloved, and lovable—and as a result the engagements with contingency are far more affective than those in the other films. This resonates with one of the images examined by Zelizer, that of Neda Agha-Soltan, a young woman who was shot and killed by a member of the state militia during the Iran uprisings of 2009. Unlike Tate's, Agha-Soltan's death unquestionably occurred as part of a larger system of state oppression. However, Zelizer notes that in addition to its uses for local resistance and global outrage, the image of Agha-Soltan's final moments triggered responses such as "arousing empathy and indignation," "imagining alternative endings," and "facilitating catharsis" (11), all of which are aspects of Tarantino's depiction of Tate in the film.

Ultimately, *Once upon a Time . . . in Hollywood* both fulfills and thwarts the viewer's desire to imagine a happy ending for Tate. As many audiences no doubt anticipated, the film does avert the Manson family's notorious murders. Unlike in *Inglourious Basterds* and *Django Unchained*, the intervention of the protagonists into the events of history in *Once upon a Time . . . in Hollywood* is completely accidental. As members of the Manson family approach the Tate-Polanski house, they are confronted by an extremely drunk Rick Dalton, who berates them for their run-down, noisy car and demands they leave. They drive a short distance away to recalibrate their plan and quickly decide that instead of the residents of 10050 Cielo Drive, they will murder famed television cowboy Rick Dalton. They return and burst into the house, but instead of Dalton they find Cliff Booth in the living room. Appropriate to his occupation as a stuntman, Booth stands in for Dalton at this moment of action. The Manson family members are dispatched in ultraviolent fashion by Booth, his exceptionally well-trained pit bull Brandy, and finally Dalton himself—armed with the flame thrower he kept as a souvenir from the film-within-a-film pastiche of *Inglourious Basterds*, *The Fourteen Fists of McCluskey*.

After the carnage, the film reaches what feels like its natural end point. The police arrive to take statements from Dalton and Booth, and Booth, who has sustained injuries, is loaded into an ambulance. In spite of his injuries, he is cheerful, asking Dalton to bring him bagels in the morning and make sure Brandy is not too shaken by the experience. Dalton watches the ambulance and police cars drive away and stands in the middle of the now-quiet street. He is centered in a medium long shot facing away from the camera. Most of the frame is in darkness, as it is still the middle of the night, and there is no sound except for crickets and Dalton's somewhat restless sigh. However, rather than ending, the film cuts to a medium length version of the same shot, and a man's voice calls "Hello?" from off screen. Dalton turns and sees Jay Sebring standing behind the Tate-Polanski security gate. Sebring is at a distance—his face obscured by the bars of the gate and the nighttime darkness around him. A small but friendly figure almost lost in the middle of the frame, he recognizes Rick Dalton from television and asks him what happened. Their conversation is shot in a series of shot-reverse-shots that consistently include the bars of the security gate separating them. Dalton stands at the end of the Tate-Polanski driveway and is initially shown in long shots that keep the gate's bars in the foreground, emphasizing his physical removal from Sebring. As the two connect and Dalton is clearly pleased that Sebring is familiar with his work, his shots become mediums that do not include the bars. However, Sebring remains inside the gate, and all the shots of him (which are consistently medium shots throughout the exchange) continue to include it.

The sound of static comes from off screen, and the cameras pan right to the security gate's call box as Dalton turns toward it. Tate's voice comes across the intercom asking, "Jay, honey, is everything all right?" Sebring reassures her that everyone is fine and tells her that he has been talking to her next-door neighbor. Tate's voice then greets Dalton, saying, "Hello, neighbor. Everybody OK?" At this, Dalton finally moves from the sidewalk into the driveway, standing close to the call box so that he can greet Tate and reassure her that he and his wife are fine. She invites him "to come up to the house for a drink and meet my other friends." Dalton glances toward Sebring, who gives him a thumbs up. For an actor who has been on the brink of struggling throughout the film, and who initially hoped that his proximity to the Tate-Polanski residence would provide a networking opportunity for him, this is the best possible outcome of any night. He politely accepts, and Sharon says she will buzz him up.

The creaky sound of the gates opening is accompanied by eerie instrumental music and a brief shot of Sebring standing motionless as the gates slowly part to allow Dalton access to his Hollywood dream space. The two shake hands and Sebring claps Dalton on the shoulder, their conversation fading as they walk up the driveway into the flowery bushes and shadows of the driveway. The camera begins to move, but rather than following the two to the house, it travels up and around the edge of the property—losing sight of them in the bushes, glancing them through the branches—until arriving at an aerial shot overlooking the Tate-Polanski driveway from the other side of the wall separating it from Dalton's home. The viewer sees Tate hug Dalton in greeting, and introduces him to her friends—people who, like Tate and Sebring, are now unknowing survivors of one of the twentieth century's most famous crimes. While some snatches of their conversation are audible, the primary sound is the eerie, wistful music that continues to play. Dalton, Sebring, Tate, and the others go inside, and the camera remains with the now-empty driveway accompanied only by the instrumental music as credits appear on-screen.

The refusal to offer the viewer any kind of direct engagement with Tate, particularly visual engagement—she is seen only from a distance, and even then primarily from behind—is in some ways a refusal to offer the alternate ending that the spectacularly violent deaths of the Manson family members seem to promise. Yes, Tate, Sebring, and the others will survive, but we are not permitted to see them do it. Their stolen potential futures remain where they have always been—in individual imaginations. Rick Dalton's invitation to the home is saturated with the visual and aural markers of a dreamscape—Sebring's sudden appearance behind the gate, addressing Dalton only when he is alone; Tate's disembodied voice; the dense foliage around the driveway; the creaky gate; and the ethereal instrumental music all combine to communicate that Dalton is entering into a liminal space of possibility. The viewer, separated by

FIGURE 10 Jay Sebring accompanies Rick Dalton to meet Sharon Tate after he unknowingly helped avert her murder. (Credit: Screenshot from *Once upon a Time . . . in Hollywood*.)

fifty years in a world that followed a different series of choices, may not enter. Even here, offered a happy ending surrounded by several old friends and one eager new one, Sharon Tate remains one of the most potent symbols of liminality—a pregnant woman. In spite of the affective yearning for a different path of history the film seeks to engender, we are never granted the catharsis of seeing her exit that liminal space and become a parent.

Conclusion

Each of the works examined here uses a dramatic departure from audience expectations of history to intervene in the historical imaginary and to challenge widely held conceptions of the past. While there is no guarantee of their effectiveness in shifting the perspective of individual viewers, they provide a means of engaging with history and challenging the status quo of the historical imaginary in ways unavailable to traditional methods of history. By conceiving of the possible trajectory of the past in unexpected ways, these alternate history works may teach audiences new ways of thinking about both the events of the past and their reverberations in the present moment. Perhaps most effectively, they insist to the viewer that history is not inert or inevitable—our shared past is the result of numerous choices that could have been made differently, and (particularly in *Inglourious Basterds* and *Django Unchained*) that we should be allowed to feel rage not only at those who perpetrated history's atrocities but also those who failed to act against them. All depict the trajectory of history not as shaped primarily by the actions of powerful individuals (either villainous or admirable) but as determined by the action or inaction of individuals with a wide variety of motivations and unpredictable impacts. In this, they encourage us to find new understandings of the present moment through a more critical engagement with the past. These are by no means perfect works—*Django Unchained* disregards the potential of women in the past to have been anything other than a man's motivating object of desire, and *Once upon a Time . . . in Hollywood* reinscribes the dominance of white masculinity into the past even as it seeks to rewrite it. However, they do provide a reworking of the dynamic between historical imaginary, mass media, and history that offers one potential pathway to new understandings of the relationship between past and present.

Conclusion

• •

On July 3, 2020, the smash hit Broadway musical *Hamilton*, which had been filmed during live shows four years earlier while most of the original cast was still performing, premiered on the streaming service Disney Plus. Writing for the *Washington Post*, Steven Zeitchik marveled that "any more cultural or economic meaning could be wrung out of *Hamilton*" given that "the rap-driven Broadway musical about the Founding Fathers and Mothers that opened in 2015 swept the Tonys, sold out soundtracks and world tours, grossed more than half a billion dollars in New York alone and ignited a full-blown renaissance for Broadway musicals among teenagers." However, the timing of *Hamilton*'s streaming debut allowed the show to be part of both a typical Fourth of July discourse about the Founding Fathers and a shared media experience for millions of Americans eager for something to enjoy and connect over during the COVID-19 pandemic. Once again, *Hamilton* was a hit, and discourse around its portrayal of the Founding Fathers revealed a number of fissures in the historical imaginary.

The fact that Americans, by and large, know relatively little American history has become a clichéd observation. It is a fact that generates much hand-wringing, as in Max Boot's opinion piece in the *Washington Post*, "Americans' Ignorance of History is a National Scandal," or Saba Naseem's "How Much U.S. History Do Americans Actually Know? Less Than You Think" for the *Smithsonian Magazine*. It is also a favorite subject of comedy, as in the College-Humor parody trailer for a fictional film about the War of 1812 that repeatedly emphasizes Americans' lack of knowledge about that conflict. When asked where he is going, the lead character initially responds, "Out west," before doubting himself and adding, "Maybe really far south. It could be Canada. You know what? I might have to go out to sea." At the end he falls to his knees in a pastiche of a dramatic war film cliché and calls out, "What happened in this time?" in despair ("War or 1812"). These and countless other examples illustrate what a vacuum of shared knowledge a work like *Hamilton* suddenly occupies when it becomes popular. Although it includes highly recognizable names of Founding Fathers in its cast (e.g., George Washington, Thomas Jefferson, and its "ten dollar Founding Father" title character), mainstream audiences possess minimal, if any, knowledge about the majority of events the musical dramatizes.

In an interview on *The Late Show with Stephen Colbert*, Lin-Manuel Miranda, *Hamilton*'s creator, described the process of mounting the musical for a London audience. He recalls, "They were all very like, 'You know, we don't know American history. I don't know how it will play.' And I was like, '*We don't know American history*. You're fine'" ("Lin-Manuel Miranda on *Hamilton*"). Miranda looks straight at the camera and energetically strikes the arm of his chair for emphasis as he makes this pronouncement of Americans' lack of historical knowledge. However, he does not engage with how *Hamilton*'s fans then adopt the show's fictionalized depiction of the past as history. But like the works examined across this book's chapters, *Hamilton* stands at the intersection of the historical imaginary, mass media, and history. As such, no amount of flagging itself as fictionalized—through contemporary musical styles, a highly diverse cast, staging elements, or Miranda's public discussions of ahistorical writing choices he made for the sake of drama—discredit it as a pedagogical resource among fans. Writing for *The Root*, Panama Jackson notes that after repeat viewings of *Hamilton*, "I randomly catch myself saying 'John Adams' with a sneer and disgust." He explains, "I literally don't know jack shit about President John Adams except he was the second president and had a son (or nephew? I should look this up) who would become the fourth president named John Quincy Adams. But because of the King, I feel like John Adams was probably wacksauce."

In my role as an educator, I have been able to observe the impact of *Hamilton*'s streaming release on the historical imaginary among my students. In the fall 2020 semester, discussion in one of my course sections wandered sufficiently that one student felt it was now on topic to declare that the real-life Alexander Hamilton and John Laurens had certainly been lovers. This turned out to be a relatively popular position in the room, created entirely by Anthony Ramos's and Lin-Manuel Miranda's performances in *Hamilton*. This was not an interpretation limited to *Hamilton* fans who had found their way to my classroom. In a humorous article in *The Root* titled "A List of Characters in *Hamilton* Who Also Should've Shot Alexander Hamilton in the Face," Damon Young includes John Laurens with the explanation that Laurens "should've shot him in the face for marrying Eliza and pining for Angelica when John was clearly in love with him and *literally right there* [emphasis in original] whispering 'Let's Have Another Round Tonight' in his ear.'"

Like many discussions of *Hamilton* the musical, the comments on Young's article include a thread debating the "truth" about Alexander Hamilton, the person. One commenter, under the username Whiggly, writes, "A fun fact from a NYTimes treatment of the historical accuracy of Hamilton the musical is that the previous major depiction of Alexander Hamilton was a 1943 play depicting him as a proto-fascist trying to install an aristocracy. So, yeah, he was likely a fairly divisive figure depending on your vision of the new country." One response to this comment notes, "The book by Ron Chernow that Miranda pulled most of his story from has been criticized by a lot of scholars for its soft touch about the less palatable parts of Hamltion's [*sic*] life. In truth, Hamltion's [*sic*] personal ambition turned him into a straight up plutocrat. . . . Lin-Manuel Miranda can write a very good show, but it's more fantasy than truth." A different respondent to Whiggly argued, "Well he was a monarchist. So turning him to a proto fascist isn't too much of a leap of faith," which earned the rejoinder from a final commenter, "Dude had to be literally talked down from shooting people who called him a monarchist."

Certainty exists in the historical imaginary in a way it cannot in history. The various commenters arguing about who Alexander Hamilton really was in response to a discussion of the mediated and fictionalized musical *Hamilton* here are a reasonable representation of a typical online discussion of either one, which now inevitably demands acknowledgment of the other. What these commenters, like my students who expressed their interest in Alexander Hamilton's love life, are seeking is an understanding of the past where the security with which narratives are presented in the historical imaginary can be offered by the discipline of history. That this is not actually the purview of the academic discipline of history is rarely, if ever, noted. The historical imaginary trains individuals to expect concrete and inarguable reports in their discussions of the past, as exemplified by the characterization of Lucy in *Timeless*. "Here," the historical imaginary promises, "is what happened. See it, feel it, enjoy it, and consume it. Here is something to *know*—about the past, and about yourself." Against that, the complex work of archival research and competing interpretations in history faces an intense, uphill battle in puncturing the historical imaginary's totalizing narratives and attempting to break free of the subordinate position it typically occupies in the constellation of historical imaginary, mass media, and history.

But the antipathy that the historical imaginary's most ardent adherents hold for history goes beyond the fact that the historical imaginary comfortably smooths over the unknowable wrinkles and contradictions of the past that history leaves intact. Although the American historical imaginary is often presented as representing history, as this book has demonstrated again and again, it does not. Instead, it is the narrative of America's past that has been created for the purpose of shaping an idealized past for an idealized national identity. When history threatens to disrupt this narrative, no matter how well documented its errors are, the historical imaginary pushes back—forcefully. The identity category of "American" is deeply rooted in the historical imaginary, and many find the moments when history attempts to correct its narratives existentially threatening. Undoubtedly this is why debates around how schools will teach American history are so strident and take the view of historians into account so minimally.

Debates over whether teachings of American history should prioritize accuracy or national pride came sharply to the foreground of national discourse in 2021, when conservative politicians and pundits began using "critical race theory" as a catchall term to describe any form of K-12 education that dealt accurately with current or historical racial inequality in the United States. Senator Ted Cruz insisted, "Critical race theory says every white person is a racist. Critical race theory says America's fundamentally racist and irredeemably racist. Critical race theory seeks to turn us against each other and if someone has a different color skin, seeks to make us hate that person" (Kruse). On his *Fox News* program, conservative pundit Tucker Carlson referred to critical race theory as a "civilization-ending poison" and called for "get[ting] cameras in the classroom, as we put them on the chests of police officers," putting "a civilian review board in every town in America to oversee the people teaching your children, forming their minds" to guarantee it is banned from classrooms (Porter).

Hysterical misdefinitions of critical race theory have been consistently debunked since they entered circulation; nearly every article reporting on the controversy includes an explanation that critical race theory is a forty-year-old, graduate-level body of theory that seeks to interrogate the ways in which racial injustice is both systemic and endemic in the United States in structures like the legal system. It is rarely taught even at the college undergraduate level and is essentially impossible to implement in K-12 schools (not that anyone is trying). But this reality has apparently done nothing to slow the tide of conservative lawmakers doing all they can to use the excuse of a wholly invented intellectual boogeyman to legislate against teaching American children unpleasant truths from America's past. In an article on the controversy written for *Time* in July 2021, Olivia Waxman notes legislative action that had already been taken: the Florida Board of Education "approved a rule that instruction 'may not define American history as something other than the creation of a new nation based largely on universal principles stated in the Declaration of Independence'"; "under a bill that was proposed in Arizona, teachers could have been fined $5,000 for teaching students to feel 'guilt over their race"; and "in a legally binding opinion, Montana's attorney general called critical race theory and antiracism training 'discriminatory' and illegal." This is an overt attempt to erase uncomfortable truths from national consciousness in service of a unified, white national identity. In the same article, Waxman points out that the American Historical Association and Fairleigh Dickinson University found in a national poll that "84% of Republican respondents said the goal [of teaching history] was to celebrate it."

In just the few months since their passage, anti–critical race theory laws have been used to threaten, punish, and even fire educators and administrators who attempt to make racial justice and diversity a part of their curricula. In Texas, James Whitfield, principal of Colleyville Heritage High School, was suspended by the district after he was accused at a school board meeting of favoring critical race theory. Whitfield, the first Black principal in his school's history, was not given an explanation or an opportunity to defend himself. As reported by the *Washington Post*, "Whitfield denied the allegations that he is promoting critical race theory at his high school" (Shepherd). Matt Hawn, who taught a contemporary issues course at Sullivan Central High School in Tennessee, was fired after assigning students an article by Ta-Nehisi Coates and showing Kyla Jenée Lacey's performance of the poem "White Privilege" (Green). In Texas, the Carroll Independent School District officially reprimanded a fourth-grade teacher because an anti-racist book was in her classroom. This led to an administrator telling teachers "they had to provide materials that presented an 'opposing' perspective of the Holocaust" (Lopez). Legislators and administrators denied that Texas's anti–critical race theory law demanded any such thing, but in insisting that a nonexistent "both sides" be taught about the history of American racism, it is hardly surprising that they unintentionally crafted policy that was interpreted to demand "both sides" be taught about all global atrocities.

Early childhood education in the United States is such that, for the vast majority of children, first encounters with information about the nation's past occur almost exclusively through the historical imaginary. Lessons commonly taught in preschools and elementary schools about such topics as Christopher Columbus, the first Thanksgiving, George Washington and the cherry tree, and numerous others are well-known and easily discredited falsehoods. It cannot surprise us that Americans know so little of their own history when the past that they are first taught to revere is entirely imagined. The historical imaginary is deeply embedded in American culture and is a significant component of national identity. It cannot be eliminated or completely displaced by history—the historical imaginary, mass media, and history are too bound up and intertwined to be teased apart. But the historical imaginary could be reshaped to allow for the formation of meaningful, empathetic relations to our shared past and its connection to our present moment. Understanding and exploring the historical imaginary as a useful inroad to meaningfully taking up Walter Benjamin's challenge to historians in "On the Concept of History;" reconsidering Americans' relationship to history is the best way to "seize hold" of the unresolved past traumas that will otherwise continue to "flash up."

Acknowledgments

I am thankful for the opportunities I had to present and discuss elements of this work with the communities at the 2016, 2018, and 2019 Film and History Conferences as well as the 2019 Society for Cinema and Media Studies Conference. This book began as my PhD dissertation and would not have been possible without the hard work and dedication of my committee: Dr. Alison Landsberg, Dr. Denise Albanese, and Dr. Jessica Scarlata. Their questions, challenges, and encouragement benefited this project immeasurably.

To describe Alison Landsberg solely as the chair of my dissertation committee would be to profoundly understate the impact she has had on the trajectory of my work and life. During the years of my PhD studies and work, she was a mentor who provided support, challenges, encouragement, and goals to chase. Alison always knew whether I needed reassurance or a push to propel me forward, and she never failed to provide either. The opportunity to learn from someone who always makes you feel empowered without ever letting you off easy is one of the best gifts a graduate student can receive, and I will always be grateful to Alison for giving it to me. I feel fortunate to have her example to aspire to.

In growing this work for publication I was fortunate to work with the editorial team at Rutgers University Press, who have consistently been professional, responsive, and encouraging. I am grateful to my reviewers for providing concrete and actionable feedback that strengthened this work's argumentation and clarity. This work also benefited significantly from the feedback of Dr. Craig Willse as I worked through the transition from dissertation to book.

I am lucky to have had the opportunity to write this book while teaching at the College of Charleston. I want to thank Dr. Jenifer Kopfman, who served as the chair of the Department of Communication during my work on this book, and Dr. Kris de Welde, the director of the Women's and Gender Studies program, who are skilled and compassionate leaders. I have loved teaching in both departments, and I could not hope for kinder, more encouraging colleagues than the ones at the College of Charleston. I am also grateful to my students, whose energy and curiosity have frequently reinvigorated my own inquiries.

The family of friends formed by my cohort in the Cultural Studies program at George Mason University was indispensable at every turn in the PhD and book process. We studied together through coursework, cheered each other through proposals, and have never missed an opportunity to build each other up. I am especially grateful for Christine Rosenfeld and Ashley Gaddy, whose advice, friendship, and example have meant the world to me in these years. I am thankful beyond words that my PhD studies brought Megan Fariello, whose friendship has been an endless gift, into my life. Conferences, publications, due dates, and numerous other challenges have all felt achievable because I undertook them with her at my side.

Finally, the support of my family has been essential to me throughout the years of this work; their love and belief in me have propelled me through every challenge—particularly my best friend, partner, and husband, Angus, who never fails to see strength and value in me. Thank you for being exactly what I need. Thank you to my parents, who have supported and cultivated my interests since childhood and have always made me feel that my voice has importance and power: it has been a gift of inestimable value. I must also express my gratitude to my grandma, whose bottomless reservoir of love and pride has buoyed me on countless days throughout my life. She made learning and literature part of our family's foundational values, and I wanted to thank her for that gift by completing a book of my own.

Works Cited

Andrewes, William J. H. "Chronicle of Timekeeping." *Scientific American*, 1 Feb. 2006, https://www.scientificamerican.com/article/a-chronicle-of-timekeeping-2006-02/.

Autry, Robyn. "Trump's '1776 Commission' Tried to Rewrite U.S. History. Biden Had Other Ideas." *NBC*, 21 Jan. 2021. https://www.nbcnews.com/think/opinion/trump-s-1776-commission-tried-rewrite-u-s-history-biden-ncna1255086.

Barthes, Roland. "Myth Today." *Mythologies*, translated by Annette Lavers, Farrar, Straus and Giroux, 1972, pp. 109–159.

Bhabha, Homi. "Of Mimicry and Man: The Ambivalence of Colonial Discourse." *October*, vol. 28, 1984, pp. 125–133.

Bell, Christopher. "Bring on the Female Superheroes!" *TED*, Oct. 2015.

Benjamin, Walter. "Theses on the Philosophy of History." In *Illuminations: Essays and Reflections*, edited by Hannah Arendt. Schocken Books, 1969.

———. *The Work of Art in the Age of Its Technological Reproducibility and Other Writings on Media*, edited by Michael W. Jennings, Brigid Doherty, and Thomas Y. Levin. Belknap Press of Harvard University Press, 2008.

Benoit, Julien. "Racism Is Behind Outlandish Theories about Africa's Ancient Architecture." 17 Sept. 2017, *The Conversation*, https://theconversation.com/racism-is-behind-outlandish-theories-about-africas-ancient-architecture-83898.

Berlant, Lauren. *The Anatomy of National Fantasy: Hawthorne Utopia, and Everyday Life*. U of Chicago P, 1991.

Bevil, Dewayne. "Trump Role Unknown in Disney's Refurbished Hall of Presidents." *Orlando Sentinel*, 19 Feb. 2017, https://www.orlandosentinel.com/travel/attractions/theme-park-rangers-blog/os-et-disney-hall-presidents-trump-20170216-story.html.

Black, Riley. "The Idiocy, Fabrications, and Lies of Ancient Aliens." *Smithsonian Magazine*, 11 May 2012, https://www.smithsonianmag.com/science-nature/the-idiocy-fabrications-and-lies-of-ancient-aliens-86294030/.

Blake, Meredith. "Why *The Great British Baking Show* Is Too Good for This Cruel, Cruel World." *Los Angeles Times*, 24 Sept. 2016, https://www.latimes.com/entertainment/tv/la-et-st-great-british-baking-show-mary-berry-leaving-20160922-snap-story.html.

Boot, Max. "Americans' Ignorance of History Is a National Scandal." *The Washington Post*, 20 Feb. 2019, https://www.washingtonpost.com/opinions/americans

-ignorance-of-history-is-a-national-scandal/2019/02/20/b8be683c-352d-11e9
-854a-7a14d7fec96a_story.html.

Bradner, Eric. "Conway: Trump White House Offered 'Alternative Facts' on Crowd Size." *CNN Politics*, 23 Jan. 2017, https://www.cnn.com/2017/01/22/politics /kellyanne-conway-alternative-facts/index.html.

"Brad Pitt & Quentin Tarantino Interview 'Inglourious Basterds.'" *YouTube*, uploaded by Jack Traven, 21 Oct. 2014, https://www.youtube.com/watch?v=y5trE0jZZ1Y.

Broggie, Michael. *Walt Disney's Railroad Story: The Small-Scale Fascination That Led to a Full-Scale Kingdom*. Pentrex, 1997.

Bruckner, René Thoreau. "'Why Did You Have to Turn On the machine?': The Spirals of Time Travel Romance." *Cinema Journal*, vol. 54, no. 2, 2015, pp. 1–23.

Burgoyne, Robert. *The Hollywood Historical Film*. Wiley-Blackwell, 2008.

Campbell-Dollaghan, Kelsey. "Celebration, Florida: The Utopian Town That America Just Couldn't Trust." *Gizmodo*, 20 Apr. 2014, https://gizmodo.com/celebration florida-the-utopian-town-that-america-jus-1564479405.

Canedo, Nick. "College Board Revise Controversial AP U.S. History Framework." *Central NY News*, 3 Oct. 2014, https://www.syracuse.com/news/index.ssf/2014 /10/college_board_revises_controversial_ap_history_framework.html.

Caro, Robert. "When LBJ Said, 'We Shall Overcome,'" *The New York Times*, 28 Aug. 2008, https://www.nytimes.com/2008/08/28/opinion/28ihtedcaro.1.15715378.html.

Carlsten, Jennie and Fearghal McGarry. *Film, History and Memory*. Palgrave MacMillan, 2015.

Corcoran, Nina. "Bruce Lee's Daughter Says Quentin Tarantino Should 'Shut Up' or 'Apologize' for Father's Portrayal." *Consequence of Sound*, 15 Aug. 2019, https:// consequenceofsound.net/2019/08/bruce-lee-quentin-tarantino-shannon-lee -once-upon-a-time-drama/?new=true.

Corn, Joseph, and Brian Horrigan. *Yesterday's Tomorrows: Past Visions of the American Future*. John Hopkins UP, 1984.

Davis, Julie Hirschfeld. "Yes, Slaves Did Help Build the White House." *The New York Times*, 26 July 2016, https://www.nytimes.com/2016/07/27/us/politics/michelle -obama-white-house-slavery.html?smid=tw-share.

de Groot, Jerome. *Consuming History: Historians and Heritage in Contemporary Popular Culture*. Routledge, 2009.

———. *Remaking History: The Past in Contemporary Historical Fictions*. Routledge, 2016.

Django Unchained. Directed by Quentin Tarantino, performances by Jamie Foxx, Christoph Waltz, Leonardo DiCaprio, and Samuel L. Jackson, Columbia Pictures, 2012.

Dwyer, Neil. "Disney Guts 'Politically Incorrect' Scene from Pirates of the Caribbean Ride." *Washington Examiner*, 4 July 2017, https://www.washingtonexaminer.com /red-alert-politics/disney-guts-politically-incorrect-scene-pirates-caribbean-ride.

Dyer, Richard. *Pastiche*. Routledge, 2006.

———. *White: Essays on Race and Culture*. Routledge, 1997.

Easley, Jonathan. "Majority of Republicans Say 2020 Election Was Invalid." *The Hill*, 25 Feb. 2021, https://thehill.com/homenews/campaign/540508-majority-of -republicans-say-2020-election-was-invalid-poll.

Ebiri, Bilge. "So, How Much of *Once upon a Time in Hollywood* Is Margot Robbie Actually In?" *Vulture*, 25 July 2019, https://www.vulture.com/2019/07/on-margot -robbies-role-in-once-upon-a-time-in-hollywood.html.

Edgerton, Gary. "Ken Burns's America." *Journal of Popular Film and Television*, vol. 21, no. 2, 1993, p. 50.

11.22.63. Created by Bridget Carpenter, Bad Robot Productions & Warner Bros. Television, 2016.

Elsaesser, Thomas. *Weimar Cinema and After: Germany's Historical Imaginary*. Routledge, 2000.

"Epcot Origins (The World Showcase)." *Disney D23*, 1 Oct. 2012, https://d23.com /from-the-archives-epcot-origins-the-world-showcase/.

Fernández Buey, Francisco. *Reading Gramsci*. Translated by Nicholas Gray. Koninkli-jke Brill, 2015.

Fortin, Jacey. "Man Inspired by TV Show *Forged in Fire* Sets Off Huge Blaze, Officials Say." *The New York Times*, 2 Dec. 2017, https://www.nytimes.com/2017/12/02 /nyregion/fire-upstate-new-york.html.

Francaviglia, Richard. "Walt Disney's Frontierland as an Allegorical Map of the American West." *Western Historical Quarterly*, vol. 30, no. 2, 1999, pp. 155–182.

Gallagher, Catherine. "War, Counterfactual History, and Alternate-History Novels." *Field Day Review*, vol. 3, 2007, pp. 52–65.

Giroux, Henry. "Memory and Pedagogy in the 'Wonderful World of Disney': Beyond the Politics of Innocence." In *From Mouse to Mermaid: The Politics of Film, Gender, and Culture*, edited by Elizabeth Bell, Lynda Haas, and Laura Sells. Indiana UP, 1995, pp. 43–61.

Glantz, Tracy. "3 Years Later, Confederate Flag Casts Shadow Again over SC State House." *The State*, 10 July 2018, https://www.thestate.com/news/politics -overnment/article214555950.html.

Gleick, James. *Time Travel: A History*. Pantheon, 2016.

Gordon, Andrew. "'Back to the Future': Oedipus as Time Traveler." *Science Fiction Studies*, vol. 14, no. 3, 1987, pp. 372–385.

Green, Emma. "He Taught a Ta-Nehisi Coates Essay. Then He Was Fired." *The Atlantic*, 17 Aug. 2021, https://www.theatlantic.com/politics/archive/2021/08 /matt-hawn-tennessee-teacher-fired-white-privilege/619770/.

Greenwood, Max. "Trump on Removing Confederate Statues: 'They're Trying to Take Away Our Culture.'" *The Hill*, 22 Aug. 2017, https://thehill.com/homenews /administration/347589-trump-on-removing-confederate-statues-theyre-trying -to-take-away-our.

"Guest Starring John Noble." *Legends of Tomorrow*, season 3, episode 17, CW, 9 Apr. 2018. *Netflix*.

Hamilton. Directed by Thomas Kail, Disney, 2020.

Handler, Richard and Eric Gable. *The New History in an Old Museum: Creating the Past at Colonial Williamsburg*. Duke UP, 1997.

Harris, Aisha. "Was There Really 'Mandingo Fighting,' Like in *Django Unchained*?" *Slate*, 24 Dec. 2012, http://www.slate.com/blogs/browbeat/2012/12/24/django _unchained_mandingo_fightin_were_any_slaves_really_forced_to_fight.html.

Haselby, Sam. "What Politicians Mean When They Say the United States Was Founded as a Christian Nation." *The Washington Post*, 4 July 2017, https://www .washingtonpost.com/news/posteverything/wp/2017/07/04/what-politicians -mean-when-they-say-america-was-founded-as-a-christian-nation/?utm_term= .4324d6d74f5c.

History. https://www.history.com.

Horkheimer, Max, and Theodor Adorno. *Dialectic of Enlightenment*. Stanford UP, 2007.

Hughes, Steve. "Man Who Started Massive Cohoes Fire Gets Year in Jail." *Times Union*, 26 June 2018, https://www.timesunion.com/news/article/Man-who -accidentally-started-massive-Cohoes-fire-13024236.php.

Hughes-Warrington, Marnie. *History Goes to the Movies: Studying History on Film*. Routledge, 2006.

Hunt, Kristin. "How a Group of 70s Radicals Tried (and Failed) to Invade Disneyland." *Atlas Obscura*, 19 July 2017, https://www.atlasobscura.com/articles /disneylandyippies-1970.

The Imagineers. *The Imagineering Field Guide to the Magic Kingdom*. Disney Editions, 2005.

———. *Walt Disney Imagineering: A Behind the Dreams Look at Making More Magic Real*. Disney Editions, 2010.

Inglourious Basterds. Directed by Quentin Tarantino, performances by Christoph Waltz, Brad Pitt, and Mélanie Laurent. Universal Pictures, 2009.

Ives, Peter. *Language and Hegemony in Gramsci*. Pluto Press, 2004.

Jackson, Panama. "10 Things I Do That Make My Wife Think I'm Addicted to *Hamilton*. I Disagree; Everybody Does This Stuff, Right?" *The Root*, 10 Sept. 2020, https://verysmartbrothas.theroot.com/10-things-i-do-that-makes-my-wife-think -im-addicted-to-1845016334.

Juzwiak, Rich. "*The Blood of Emmett Till* Author Talks Interviewing Till's Accuser and Being Published alongside Milo Yiannopoulos." *Jezebel*, 30 Jan. 2017, http:// jezebel.com/the-blood-of-emmett-till-author-talks-interviewing-till-1791767529.

Karlgaard, Rich. "Seven Lessons of Walt Disney." *Forbes*, 8 Dec. 2006, https://www .forbes.com/free_forbes/2006/1225/033.html.

Katz, Jackson. "Are We Witnessing a Crisis in White Masculinity?" *Newsweek*, 14 Jan. 2019, https://www.newsweek.com/are-we-witnessing-crisis-white-male -masculinity-781048.

Koenig, David. *Realityland: True-Life Adventures at Walt Disney World*. Bonaventure Press, 2007.

Kracauer, Siegfried. *The Mass Ornament: Weimar Essays*. Edited by Thomas Y. Levin, Harvard UP, 1995.

Kruse, Kevin. "Ted Cruz's Erroneous Definition of Critical Race Theory Explains White America." *MSNBC*, 20 June 2021, https://www.msnbc.com/opinion/ted -cruz-s-erroneous-definition-critical-race-theory-explains-white-n1271484.

Kryah, Kevin. "Talking Swords on the Brooklyn Set of History's New Reality-Competition Series." *Esquire*, 23 June 2015, https://www.esquire.com /entertainment/tv/a35900/forged-in-fire/.

Kurutz, Steven. "Suspicious Minds." *The New York Times*, 21 July 2018, http://www .nytimes.com/2018/07/21/style/ancient-aliens.html.

Landsberg, Alison. *Engaging the Past: Mass Culture and the Production of Historical Knowledge*. Columbia UP, 2015.

Lang, Robert, ed. *The Birth of a Nation*. Rutgers University Press, 1994.

Le Miere, Jason. "Donald Trump Says 'Our Ancestors Tamed a Continent' and 'We Are Not Going to Apologize for America.'" *Newsweek*, 25 May 2018, https:// www.newsweek.com/donald-trump-tame-continent-america-945121.

"Lin-Manuel Miranda on *Hamilton* in the US vs. UK." *YouTube*, uploaded by The Late Show with Stephen Colbert, 17 Oct. 2018, https://www.youtube.com/watch ?v=naq6o3w88bA&t=266s.

Liston, Barbara. "Florida's Mouse behind the Curtain." *Politico Magazine*, 18 June 2015, https://www.politico.com/magazine/story/2015/06/what-works-orlando-disney -politics-119167/.

Lopez, Brian. "The Law That Prompted a School Administrator to Call for an 'Opposing' Perspective on the Holocaust Is Causing Confusion across Texas." *The Texas Tribune*, 15 Oct. 2021, https://www.texastribune.org/2021/10/15/Texas -critical-race-theory-law-confuses-educators/.

Magic Kingdom Park. Walt Disney World, 2018, https://disneyworld.disney.go.com /destinations/magic-kingdom/.

Making History. Created by Julius Sharpe. 20th Century Fox Television, 2017.

The Man Who Shot Liberty Valance. Directed by John Ford, Paramount Pictures, 1962.

Marling, Karal Ann. "Imagineering the Disney Theme Parks." In *Designing Disney's Theme Parks: The Architecture of Reassurance*, edited by Karal Ann Marling. Flammarion, 1997, pp. 29–179.

Marotta, Jenna. "Sharon Tate's Sister Met with Quentin Tarantino, Is Now More Comfortable with *Once upon a Time . . . in Hollywood*." *IndieWire*, 24 July 2018, https://www.indiewire.com/2018/07/once-upon-a-time-in-hollywood-quentin -tarantino-sharon-tate-sister-1201987556/.

Mauro, Jason Isaac. "Disney's Splash Mountain: Death Anxiety, the Tar Baby, and Rituals of Violence." *Children's Literature Association Quarterly*, vol. 22, no. 3, 1997, pp. 113–117.

Mazza, Ed. "Disney to Revamp Jungle Cruise Ride to Fix 'Negative Depictions of Natives.'" *The Huffington Post*, 26 Jan. 2021, http://huffpost.com/entry/disney -jungle-cruise-changes-native-people_n_600fbc70c5b604d2cc866a75/amp.

McIntyre, Ashton. "Woman Who Competed on Show *Alone* Speaks Out about Experience." *KSBY News*, 3 Dec. 2019, https://www.ksby.com/news/local-news /woman-who-competed-on-show-alone-speaks-out-about-experience.

Miller, Julie. "Sharon Tate's Sister Loved Margot Robbie in *Once upon a Time . . . in Hollywood*." *Vanity Fair*, 25 July 2019, https://www.vanityfair.com/hollywood /2019/07/once-upon-a-time-in-hollywood-margot-robbie-sharon-tate.

Molloy, Tim. "Bruce Lee's Daughter Saddened by 'Mockery' in *Once upon a Time . . . in Hollywood*." *The Wrap*, 29 July 2019, https://www.thewrap.com/bruce-lee -daughter-mockery-once-upon-a-time-hollywood-shannon-lee/.

Montgomery, Charles. *Happy City*. Farrar, Straus and Giroux, 2013.

Naseem, Saba. "How Much U.S. History Do Americans Actually Know? Less Than You Think." *Smithsonian Magazine*, 28 May 2015, https://www.smithsonianmag .com/history/how-much-us-history-do-americans-actually-know-less-you-think -180955431/.

National Council on Public History. "The Changing Past," https://ncph.org/what-is -public-history/how-historians-work/the-changing-past/.

Nayeri, Farah. "Quentin Tarantino Passes on Question about Screen Treatment of Margot Robbie." *The New York Times*, 22 May 2019, https://www.nytimes.com /2019/05/22/movies/quentin-tarantino-margot-robbie.html.

Norris, Luke. "Bruce Lee Once Revealed What Would Happen If He Fought Muhammad Ali." *Sportscasting.com*, 2 June 2020, https://www.sportscasting.com /bruce-lee-once-revealed-what-would-happen-if-he-fought-muhammad-ali/.

Nunnery, Stu. "I'm Walking Right Down the Middle of Main Street, U.S.A." *Disneyland Fun*, 1990.

O'Keefe, Meghan. "*Forged in Fire* Is Amped Up to Bring Female Smiths into the Spotlight in Season Two." *Decider*, 16 Feb. 2016, https://decider.com/2016/02/16

/forged-in-fire-is-amped-up-to-bring-female-smiths-into-the-spotlight-in-season
-two/.

"Our Withdrawn Review 'Blood Cotton.'" *The Economist*, 5 Sept. 2014, http://www
.economist.com/news/books/21615864-how-slaves-built-american-capitalism-blood
-cotton.

Patton. Directed by Franklin Schaffner. 20th Century Fox, 1970.

Pennell, Julie. "Disney to Clean Up Pirates of the Caribbean Ride to Make It More PC."
Today, 3 July 2017, https://www.today.com/popculture/disney-s-pirates-caribbean
-ride-lose-wench-auction-pc-makeover-t1113417.

Perrillo, Jonna. "Once Again, Texas's Board of Education Exposed How Poorly We
Teach History." *The Washington Post*, 21 Sept. 2018, https://www.washingtonpost
.com/outlook/2018/09/21/once-again-texass-board-education-exposed-how-poorly
-we-teach-history/?utm_term=.42eb0a0d13ce.

Peyser, Eve. "The Nicest Reality Show on TV Is All about Deadly Weapons." *Vice*,
15 Sept. 2017, https://www.vice.com/en/article/bjvxza/the-nicest-reality-show-on
-tv-is-all-about-deadly-weapons.

Pogrebin, Robin. "Roosevelt Statue to Be Removed from Museum of Natural History."
The New York Times, 21 June 2020, https://www.nytimes.com/2020/06/21/arts
/design/roosevelt-statue-to-be-removed-from-museum-of-natural-history.html.

Pollock, Griselda. *Vision and Difference: Feminism, Femininity and Histories of Art*.
Routledge, 2003.

Porter, Tom. "Tucker Carlson Called for Cameras in Classrooms to Make Sure
Teachers Don't Tell Kids about Critical Race Theory." *Business Insider*, 7 July 2021,
https://www.businessinsider.com/tucker-carlson-cameras-school-stop-critical-race
-theory-2021-7.

Prieur, Danielle. "Disney Revamp of Jungle Cruse Ride Removes Racist Depictions
of Indigenous People." *NPR*, 29 Jan. 2021, http://www.npr.org/2021/01/29
/962190246/disney-revamp-of-jungle-cruise-ride-removes-racist-depictions-of
-indigenous-peop.

Puchko, Kristy. "Review: *Forged in Fire* Is a Charming Challenge to Toxic Masculinity."
Pajiba, 8 Oct. 2018, https://www.pajiba.com/tv_reviews/review-forged-in-fire-is-a
-charming-challenge-to-toxic-masculinity.php.

"Quentin Tarantino, 'Unchained' and Unruly." *NPR*, 2 Jan. 2013, http://www.npr.org
/2013/01/02/168200139/quentin-tarantino-unchained-and-unruly.

Quinn, Eithne. "Sincere Fictions: The Production Cultures of Whiteness in Late
1960s Hollywood." *The Velvet Light Trap*, vol. 67, 2011, pp. 3–13.

Robson, Tom. "'The Future Is Truly in the Past': The Regressive Nostalgia of Tomorrowland." In *Performance and the Disney Theme Park Experience*, edited by Jennifer
Kokai and Tom Robson. Palgrave MacMillan, 2019, pp. 23–42.

Rosenfeld, Gavriel. *Hi Hitler! How the Nazi Past Is Being Normalized in Contemporary
Culture*. Cambridge UP, 2015.

———. "Why Do We Ask 'What If?': Reflections on the Function of Alternate
History." *History and Theory*, vol. 41, no. 4, 2002, 90–103.

Rosenstone, Robert. *History on Film/Film on History*. Routledge, 2012.

———. *Visions of the Past: The Challenge of Film to Our Idea of History*. Harvard UP,
1998.

Rymsza-Pawlowska, Malgorzata. "Broadcasting the Past: History Television, 'Nostalgia
Culture,' and the Emergence of the Miniseries in the 1970s in the United States."
Journal of Popular Film and Television, vol. 42, no. 2, 2014, pp. 81–90.

Said, Edward. "Orientalism Once More." *Development and Change*, vol. 35, no. 5, 2004, pp. 869–879.

Schone, Mark. "Media Circus: All Hitler All the Time." *Salon*, 18 May 1997, https://www.salon.com/1997/05/08/media_90/.

Scott, Eugene. "Trump's Ardent Defense of Confederate Monuments Continues as Americans Swing the Opposite Direction," *The Washington Post*, 1 July 2020, https://www.washingtonpost.com/politics/2020/07/01/trumps-ardent-defense-confederate-monuments-continues-americans-swing-opposite-direction/.

Sharf, Zack. "Quentin Tarantino Defends *Hollywood* Bruce Lee Fight from Claims It Mocks the Late Action Star." *IndieWire*, 12 Aug. 2019, https://www.indiewire.com/2019/08/quentin-tarantino-defends-bruce-lee-fight-once-upon-a-time-in-hollywood-1202165238/.

Shepherd, Kate. "Texas Parents Accused a Black Principal of Promoting Critical Race Theory: The District Has Now Suspended Him." *The Washington Post*, 1 Sept. 2021, https://www.washingtonpost.com/nation/2021/09/01/texas-principal-critical-race-theory/.

Sklar, Marty. "The Artist as Imagineer." In *Designing Disney's Theme Parks: The Architecture of Reassurance*, edited by Karal Ann Marling. Flammarion, 1997, pp. 13–18.

Smith, Ben. "Real America?" *Politico*, 6 Nov. 2008, https://www.politico.com/blogs/ben-smith/2008/11/real-america-014013.

Snelling, Sherri. "First U.S. 'Dementia Village' Recreates a Happier Time." *Forbes.com*, 26 Apr. 2017, https://www.forbes.com/sites/nextavenue/2017/04/26/first-u-sdementia-village-recreates-a-happier-time/#171741487433.

Sobchack, Vivian. *The Persistence of History: Cinema, Television, and the Modern Event*. Routledge, 1995.

———. *Screening Space: The American Science Fiction Film*. Rutgers University Press, 1997.

Sperb, Jason. *Disney's Most Notorious Film: Race, Convergence, and the Hidden Histories of Song of the South*. U of Texas P, 2013.

Surrell, Jason. *The Disney Mountains: Imagineering at Its Peak*. Disney Editions, 2007.

———. *The Haunted Mansion: Imagineering a Disney Classic*. Disney Editions, 2015.

———. *Pirates of the Caribbean: From the Magic Kingdom to the Movies*. Disney Editions, 2005.

Sylt, Christian. "The Secrets behind Disney's $2.2 Billion Theme Park Profits." *Forbes.com*, 14 July 2014, https://www.forbes.com/sites/csylt/2014/07/14/thesecrets-behind-disneys-2-2-billion-theme-park-profits/#24f6b498584f.

Taves, Brian. "The History Channel and the Challenge of Historical Programming." *Film & History: An Interdisciplinary Journal of Film and Television Studies*, vol. 30 no. 2, 2000, pp. 7–16. Project MUSE muse.jhu.edu/article/400651.

Taylor, Charles. *Modern Social Imaginaries*. Duke UP, 2003.

Timeless. Created by Eric Kripke and Shawn Ryan. Middkid Productions, 2016–2018.

Treacey, Mia. *Reframing the Past: History, Film and Television*. Routledge, 2016.

Tumulty, Karen, and Lyndsey Layton. "Changes in AP History Trigger a Culture Clash in Colorado." *The Washington Post*, 5 Oct. 2014, https://www.washingtonpost.com/politics/2014/10/05/fa6136a2-4b12-11e4-b72e d6oa9229cc10_story.html?utm_term=.3baod6d4aea.

Wallace, Mike. "Mickey Mouse History: Portraying the Past at Disney World." *Radical History Review*, vol. 32, 1985, pp. 33–57.

"The War of 1812: The Movie." *YouTube*, uploaded by CollegeHumor, 4 Oct. 2011, https://www.youtube.com/watch?v=w2AfQ5pa59A.

Wasko, Janet. "Challenging Disney Myths." *Journal of Communication Inquiry*, vol. 25, no. 3, 2001, pp. 237–257.

Waxman, Olivia. "Critical Race Theory: The Fight over What History Kids Learn." *Time*, 16 July 2021, https://time.com/6075193/critical-race-theory-debate/.

Weigel, Brandon. "This Will Kill: History Channel's *Forged in Fire* and Economic Anxiety." *The Baltimore Sun*, 5 July 2017, https://www.baltimoresun.com /citypaper/bcp-070517-screens-forged-in-fire-20170705-story.html.

Williams, Jesse. "Django, in Chains." *CNN*, 21 Jan. 2013, http://www.cnn.com/2013 /02/19/opinion/williams-django-still-chained/.

Williams, Linda. "Mega-Melodrama! Vertical and Horizontal Suspensions of the 'Classical.'" *Modern Drama*, vol. 55, no. 4, 2012, pp. 523–543.

———. *Playing the Race Card: Melodramas of Black and White from Uncle Tom to O. J. Simpson*. Princeton UP, 2001.

Williams, Raymond. *Television*. Routledge, 1974.

Wills, John. *Disney Culture*. Rutgers UP, 2017.

Wilmore, Larry. "Comedian: Why Don't Black People See UFOs?" *Today*, 9 Jan. 2009, https://www.today.com/popculture/comedian-why-don-t-black-people-see -ufoswbna28933664.

Wilson, Janelle. *Nostalgia: Sanctuary of Meaning*. Bucknell UP, 2005.

Wittenberg, David. *Time Travel: The Popular Philosophy of Narrative*. Fordham UP, 2013.

Young, Damon. "A List of Characters in *Hamilton* Who Also Should've Shot Alexander Hamilton in the Face." *The Root*, 6 Aug. 2020, https://verysmartbrothas .theroot.com/a-list-of-characters-in-hamilton-who-also-shouldve-shot-1844635902.

Zeitchik, Steven. "Why Disney Plus's July 4 Streaming of *Hamilton* Is Historic." *The Washington Post*, 24 June 2020, https://www.washingtonpost.com/business /2020/06/24/hamilton-july4-disneyplus-streaming/.

Zelizer, Barbie. *About to Die: How News Images Move the Public*. Oxford UP, 2010.

Index

About the Author

CAROLINE GUTHRIE teaches at the Department of Communication and the Women's and Gender Studies program at the College of Charleston in South Carolina. She completed her PhD in cultural studies at George Mason University. Her previous publications include "Narratives of Rupture: Tarantino's Counterfactual Histories and the American Historical Imaginary" in *Rethinking History*; "Walt Disney World: Marxism and Myth Creation" in *Proceedings of the New York State Communication Association*, and multiple articles on the website *Film-Cred*.